RELIGIOUS WARS IN THE COURTS I: THE LOWER FEDERAL COURTS AND THE U.S. SUPREME COURT IN RELIGIOUS FREEDOMS CASES 1970-1990

Religious Wars In the Courts I: The Lower Federal Courts and the U.S. Supreme Court In Religious Freedoms Cases 1970-1990

Barbara M. Yarnold, J.D., Ph.D.

Nova Science Publishers, Inc.
Huntington, NY

Editorial Production: Susan Boriotti
Office Manager: Annette Hellinger
Graphics: Frank Grucci and Jennifer Lucas
Information Editor: Tatiana Shohov
Book Production: Patrick Davin, Cathy DiGregory, Donna Dennis, Jennifer Kuenzig, Christine Mathosian, Tammy Sauter and Lynette Van Helden
Circulation: Lisa DiGangi and Michael Pazy Mino

Library of Congress Cataloging-in-Publication Data

Yarnold, Barbara M.
Religious Wars in the Courts I: The Lower Federal Courts and the U.S. Supreme Court in Religious Freedoms Cases 1970-1990 / Barbara M. Yarnold
p.cm.
Includes bibliographical references and index.
ISBN 1-56072-755-1 (v.1) – ISBN 1-56072-756-X (v.2)
1. Freedom of Religion—United States—History. 2. Religion and State—United States—History. 3. Judicial Process—United States—History.

KF4783 .Y37 1999
342.73'0852—dc21

99-052389

227 Main Street, Suite 100
Huntington, New York 11743
Tele. 631-424-6682 Fax 631-424-4666
E Mail Novascil@aol.com

Printed in the United States of America

Dedication

To Johnny (my son) and Mom, the two great loves of my life.

CONTENTS

INTRODUCTION

This analysis is concerned with two decades 1970-1990 of adjudications by the lower federal courts--district and circuit courts of appeals and the U.S. Supreme Court--in "religious freedoms" cases, or cases which relate to the 1st Amendment's "free-exercise" and "establishment" clauses. There are a number of reasons for dealing with these two clauses simultaneously.

The first is pragmatic: most judicial decisions which deal with religious liberties discuss both clauses. Second, from a more theoretical perspective, the free exercise and establishment clauses share a common purpose, namely protecting the liberties of religious individuals and the non-religious. Finally, it is based upon an underlying skepticism about the importance of rules, and even the existence of rules, concepts which have emerged in the public law area and among legal realists.

SCIENTIFIC OBJECTIVES OF THE STUDY

The project draws upon the Yarnold's prior work in the public law area, which has been concerned with the question of why federal court outcomes are related to political factors (including interest group involvement in litigation, the partisanship of judges, and the preferences of judicial constituencies), and to the environment, while in other types of cases political factors do not reach the level of statistical significance (Yarnold 1990a, 1990b, 1991, 1992, 1994a, 1994b 1995, 1997). Drawing upon Yarnold's research and that of others, a general theory of public law was developed (Yarnold 1992, 1995) which predicts that federal courts, in spite of lifetime appointments, are likely to respond to political factors when the case in question involves a major issue that is well-publicized and tends to divide the electorate along partisan lines. This, incidentally, is an adaptation of Page et. al's (1983) earlier work on congressional decision making. Hence, in Yarnold's previous research, asylum and refugee appeals from 1980-1987 and abortion cases adjudicated during the period 1973-1990, both dealing with major issues, the outcomes were related to political factors.

In contrast, in cases dealing with international extradition, judicial outcomes were not related to the same political factors (interest group involvement, judicial constituents, and partisanship). Although these types of cases are of immense interest to certain ethnic groups in the United States, they are not well-publicized and not likely to divide the electorate along partisan lines. Hence, international extradition is not, arguably, a major issue. However, it was observed that the individuals who were subject to extradition requests were much more likely to prevail if they were linked to the IRA, while those linked to the PLO were much less likely to prevail. It was argued that the Irish lobby in the U.S. is much stronger than the Palestinian lobby. Hence, a second part of the model predicts that other cases in which judicial outcomes may be related to political factors are those which involve non-major issues, but are nevertheless of interest to major groups in the U.S.

In most of the Yarnold's research, region was also included in the analysis. However, in asylum and international extradition cases, region was not significant. In contrast, in many analyses region has been found to be significantly related to judicial outcomes, for example, in environmental litigation (Wenner 1982; Wenner and Dutter 1988) and race relations cases (Richardson and Vines 1978). To reconcile these disparate findings, Yarnold (1995) suggested that region might be most likely to be significant in cases which deal with a highly ideological issue, such as abortion. Hence, in fact, in abortion cases, region was found to be significantly related to the outcome (Yarnold 1995).

One of the major research objectives of this study is to test, in the context of religious liberty cases (or cases which involve the free exercise or establishment clauses), clearly cases which involve major issues, the various predictions of the general theory of public law.

Specifically, are outcomes in these cases related to "political factors" (the involvement of interest groups in litigation, judicial constituents, and the partisanship of judges)? Further, since these cases are also highly ideological, are the outcomes significantly related to region? Of course, if the model is unsupported by the analysis, the hope is then to fashion a new or modified one in light of the new findings.

It is also anticipated that the power of the model will be enhanced by the addition of the "political activism" inquiry. In other words, it is anticipated that judges which were political activists prior to their ascent to the federal bench (they held political and/or appointive office), will decide the religious freedoms cases differently from those who were not political activists, although there is no specific prediction at this point about the direction of the relationship (that is, whether they will be more of less sympathetic to "religion" than their non-activist counterparts).

In an effort to further understand politically activist judges, the analysis will also evaluate whether the activists are more likely than the non-activists to render decisions which favor interest groups, are responsive to judicial constituents, and are highly partisan.

In addition to improving the political analysis of court cases, the research will also examine other facets of the judicial environment which may also help to understand decisions in cases involving religious liberties. The dependent variable in all cases is whether the judicial decision is one which is pro-religion. The additional factors which will be included relate to arguably relevant factors relating to the judges including: their religious affiliations (or lack of religious belief), their ages, and their gender.

AN IMPORTANT TECHNICAL NOTE: DATA AND METHODS

A couple of sample cases drawn from the district courts will help to introduce the data set employed in this analysis of religious freedoms cases.

In Dawson v. Mizell, 325 F.Supp. 511 (Ed. Va. 1971), a post office worker claimed that the employer, the U.S. post office, had violated the employee's free exercise rights since the employee was a 7th Day Adventist and, in violation of the tenets of that faith, was forced to work on Saturdays (the Sabbath). The case was presided over by the Honorable Robert R. Merhige, who had been appointed by Johnson in 1967, was a Catholic, had not been a political activist, and was a member of the Democratic Party. The case had no interest group involvement and was presided over by male judge who was 52 years of age at the time that the decision was rendered. The case was decided by a court in the South, in Richmond, Virginia which had a low percentage of 7th Day Adventists in the state; only .4% of the state's population were 7th Day Adventists. The decision went against the plaintiff, the court holding that there had been no violation of the free exercise rights of the 7th Day Adventist as a result of the U.S. Post Office's requiring the plaintiff to work on the Sabbath. In this case, the decision was coded anti-religion since it did not serve to advance the ability of the plaintiff to practice his or her faith.

The case of the Gilfillan v. City of Philadelphia, 480 F.Supp. 1161 (E.D. Pa., 1979), involved a taxpayer suit against the City of Philadelphia, based on the First Amendment, which sought an injunction against that city's use of public funds to construct a base that was to be used for a Papal Mass. The religion which was involved in the case was the Roman Catholic religion and the case arose in Philadelphia, Pennsylvania, in the Northeast. The plaintiff was assisted by two groups in this case, the American Civil Liberties Union and by National Ministries, American Baptist Churches in the United States of America. The presiding judge was Raymond J. Broderick who had been appointed by President Nixon in 1971, and was a Republican. The judge was a Catholic, a male, a political activist, and 65 at the time that the decision was rendered. The court found for the plaintiff, holding that the use of public funds for a Papal Mass would violate the First Amendment. Over a third (33%) of Pennsylvania's population was Catholic. The decision was coded as anti-religion once again, because it did serve to promote the free exercise rights of Roman Catholics, for whom a Papal Mass is an important religious occasion.

The dependent variable in the analysis of court cases is: is the decision beneficial to religion (a dichotomous dependent variable)? Specifically, cases usually involved one or more religious denominations and if the decision benefited the specific denomination, then the decision was coded as "pro-religion." There was no attempt to evaluate whether the decision benefited religion in a more holistic or general sense since this would lead to great difficulty in coding the dependent variable, and lend itself to inappropriate subjective "guesses" about the extent to which religion in general was benefited by a particular judicial outcome. The more conservative approach adopted here--namely limiting the analysis to whether religious individuals and organizations who were litigants in these cases prevailed--has advantages in terms of conceptual clarity and limiting the scope of the inquiry. This conservative approach, however, also had disadvantages, since a number of cases had to be excluded from the analysis as they made no specific mention of a particular religious organization.

Information on interest group involvement in the cases was derived from reading the cases, which typically list the interest groups. Information on the partisan affiliation of judges, their religions (or lack of religious affiliation), their ages, and their gender were gathered from a **Judicial Staff Directory** (Brownson 1991), and from another source book, **The American Bench** (Lichterman 1978). These sources were also be used to determine whether the judges are political activists, with judges gaining this designation if, in their pre-appointment activities, they held one or more elective or appointive office. Wenner's (1982; 1988) typology of region was used for coding the region variable in this analysis. The "judicial constituency" variable in these cases is measured as follows: the case will be scanned to determine which religion is in issue. For example, a case involving a use of public funds for a Papal Mass will be coded: Roman Catholic. Most of the cases are much more straightforward, however, involving an individual who is either filing an action or defending an action and indicates his or her religious affiliation. In other instances, as where an ordinance allows for the maintenance of a lighted cross in a public park, there is usually no specific religion involved but it will fall into the category of "general Christian." In these cases, there has been no attempt to categorize the religion. After ascertaining the religion in dispute, such as Roman Catholic, the state in which the case was adjudicated is identified. From this, the judicial constituency variable is measured as: percentage of the state population which is the religion in question. Hence if the home state of the case were Rhode Island, and the case involved Roman Catholics, a measure is made of the percentage of the population in Rhode Island in 1990 that was Catholic: 61.7% The information on the religious populations within states is derived from **Religion in Contemporary American Society**, by Kosmin and Lachman (Crown Publishers, Inc. 1993). Once again, as in the case of the dependent variable, if there is no specific mention in the case of a religious denomination, the case is excluded from the analysis.

Since the dependent variable is dichotomous (whether the outcome is pro-religion) and there are multiple independent variables, statistical analysis involved the use of probit. Probit analysis has been employed is similar research contexts. (Segal 1984; Wenner and Dutter 1988, Yarnold 1990a, 1991a.)

Chapter 1

VIEWING THE "INNER CIRCLE": DISTRICT COURT JUDGES IN RELIGIOUS FREEDOMS CASES, 1970-1990

This part focuses upon lower federal court decisions which deal with religious liberties, namely either the free exercise or non-establishment clause of the 1st Amendment to the U.S. Constitution. The time span involved is two decades, from 1970-1990. This section focuses upon the district courts.

Perhaps the greatest insight into the politicized nature of the federal courts have been offered by Baum (1989). In his work on the lower federal courts and the U.S. Supreme Court, he points out that these courts are immersed in politics in spite of the fact that they are presumably shielded from these influences due to their lifetime appointments.

However, Baum (1989) notes that these judges have, for the most part, been selected based upon their prior work for political parties, and that almost all of the judges are of the same political party as their appointing Presidents. He went on to analyze characteristics of typical federal judges and found that most of these judges have held political and/or appointive office prior to their selection to the federal judiciary.

In this twenty-year survey of federal district court judges involved in religious freedoms cases, the same observations hold. Namely, federal court judges had often, for example served as state court judges, served either in state legislatures or in Congress, or served as the Attorney Generals for their states. Further, this politicized activity was the rule rather than the exception. This study classified district court judges as a "political activists" if they had held one or more political or appointive office prior to their appointment. Three-quarters (75%) of the judges were found to be political activists. Those who were not activists were often private attorneys with distinguished records, many of whom had held positions on bar organizations external to mainstream U.S. politics. Hence, they were legal activists rather than political activists. There was the occasional law professor who was also appointed who was not a political activist.

Given the fact that most of these judges had long careers in partisan politics prior to their appointment to the federal bench, it is not surprising that they are not a particularly young group. For the federal district court judges that adjudicated religious freedoms cases during the period 1970-1990, the average age was 59 years of age.

In spite of the fact that in recent years, women roughly equal men in numbers in terms of admissions to law schools, in the religious freedoms cases surveyed here, 95% of the judges were men, while only 5% were women. On the other hand, the judges were evenly split in terms of their partisanship, with 50% of the judges being members of the Democratic Party, while 50% were Republicans.

Given the salience of these issues to major organized religious groups, it is not surprising there was heavy involvement in these cases of pro-religion interest groups, or groups who supported the 1st Amendment rights of a particular religion. Thirty-eight percent of these cases involved pro-religion groups. The pro-religion groups included not only religious organizations, but other actors, such as civil liberties groups. Since some of these cases involved indigent prisoners who claimed their religious rights had been violated by prison officials, legal aid groups often also made their appearance, as well as ad-hoc citizens groups which argued that, for example, the public schools were violating the religious freedoms of their students.

Twenty-two percent of the religious freedoms cases also involved anti-religion groups, and these included, for example, civil liberties groups, organizations committed to preventing the intermixture of religion with public institutions, labor unions which argued that workers should be forced to pay union dues and/or join unions in spite of the fact that their religions proscribed such activities, and teacher's unions that battled to ensure that funds allocated to public schools should be restricted to public schools and not expended on religious schools.

The religion cases occurred most often in the Midwest (30% of the cases) and the North (30% of the cases). Southern states were included in 22% of the cases, while only 12% of the cases were adjudicated in the West.

In terms of the religious backgrounds of the judges, 62% indicated that they belong to a religious denomination, leaving about 38% non-religious. In terms of their rank, Catholic judges were the most prevalent, appearing in 17% of the cases, followed, in descending order, by Episcopalians (9%) Presbyterians and Methodists (both at 8%), Jewish judges (5%), Protestants (4%), Baptists (3%), Lutherans and Christians (both at 2%), and then tied at the one percent or lower level are judges who belong to the following denominations: Disciples of Christ, Latter Day Saints, Congregationalist, and Community Church.

Chapter 2

DID ACTIVIST DISTRICT JUDGES DECIDE CASES INVOLVING RELIGIOUS LIBERTIES DIFFERENTLY THAN NON-ACTIVIST JUDGES? 1970-1990

This project evaluates, for the period of 1970-1990, decision making by the federal courts in cases which concern religious liberties, protected by the First Amendment of the U.S. Constitution. Specifically, the analysis concentrates on federal court cases which deal with the free exercise and establishment clauses of the First Amendment.

The research is at the district court level, and examines whether activist judges were more likely than non-activist judges to render decisions in these cases that were responsive to the partisanship of the judges, the participation of both pro- and anti-religion groups, and the judicial constituencies which are represented in these cases.

RELIGIOUS FREEDOMS AND THE FEDERAL COURTS

Unlike the other "fundamental" rights contained in the First Amendment to the U.S. Constitution, including freedom of speech, press and assembly, which are arguably necessary to the functioning of a representative democracy, the free exercise and establishment clauses of the same amendment are fundamental not due to political necessity but due to historical accident: the fact that so many of the colonists had fled religious persecution in other countries. This is not meant to imply that the religious freedoms clauses of the First Amendment are secondary in any way to the others, it is instead to suggest the vital importance of religious liberty in our constitutional schema, grounded as it is in our nation's history, customs, and political culture.

Although immigrants to the United States may have often been united in their search for religious freedom, it has also been the case that religious differences in this country have led to division. Religious groups were often segregated economically, politically, socially, and even geographically (Kosmin and Lachman 1993). Underlying the debate were fundamental questions which were to guide men and women to truth, morality, justice, and knowledge of their creator. Each religious group unfortunately, tended to answer these fundamental questions with highly or slightly idiosyncratic principles. As a result, debates within the religious community were often filled with friction. To make matters worse, also entering the debate were those who insisted that they had no religious belief and did not want the state to proselytize them in any manner.

The federal courts were given the task of making order out of this disorder, through their apolitical, objective, and almost scientific interpretation of the free exercise and establishment clauses of the First Amendment. Needless to say, their interpretations of the religious freedoms clauses in specific cases has engendered even more debate, within the legal community, among legal scholars,

among the press, policy makers, and the general public. Not surprisingly, there are many critics. And the criticism seems to be warranted at times, when after reviewing cases in perhaps a course on constitutional law, one finds that the rules which emanate from the federal courts in cases dealing with religious freedoms seem to change, are often unclear, conflicting, and impossible to reconcile. A frantic law student studying for a test may surmise unhappily, "perhaps there are no rules."

Although the legal community has been quite thorough in its doctrinal analysis of court cases involving religious liberties (Tribe 1988, Gey 1990, Laycock 1991, Brown 1993, Choper 1995), the same cannot be said of the public law area. To date, relatively few public law analyses of cases involving the free exercise and establishment clauses of the First Amendment have been conducted. Another general observation is that much of the research in the public law area has focused upon the U.S. Supreme Court, and not on the lower federal courts (Shapiro 1993). There have been few, if any, similar analyses of whether activist federal district court judges are more or less responsive in their decision making than non-activist judges to their partisan affiliations, the involvement of pro-and anti-religion groups, and the presumed desires of their judicial constituents. For these reasons, the proposed research is not likely to be redundant.

The research utilizes for its purposes federal district court cases which deal with the free exercise and establishment clauses.

Data and Methods

Official Reporters (the Federal Supplement) were used to gather cases for this analysis. The cases included here are for two decades, from 1970 to 1990. The total data set is 663 district court cases decided during this period. The dependent variable is: is the judge an activist (a dichotomous dependent variable)? Information on judicial activism is gathered from Judicial Staff Directory (Brownson 1991), and from another source book, The American Bench (Lichterman 1978). Once again, judges were deemed to be activists if they had held one or more political and/or appointive offices prior to their appointment to the federal bench.

The independent variables relating to partisanship, pro-religion interest group litigation, anti-religion interest group litigation, and the preferences of judicial constituents, were coded in the following manner. The judge was deemed to have responded to his or her party ties if he or she were a Republican judge and decided the case in a pro-religion manner, and if he or she were a Democratic judge and decided the case in an anti-religion manner. For the pro-interest group measure, judges were deemed to have entered a pro-religious group decision in a case if the pro-religion group won the case (and a pro-religion decision was entered). Anti-religious groups were also recorded as being successful litigants if they won their case (and thus an anti-religion decision was entered). To compute the judicial constituency measure, for each case, a measure was taken of the religious affiliations that were involved in the case, for example, Mormons. Since each district court is located within a state, a measure was taken of the percentage of that state's population which shares the same religion as the one involved in the case. For example, if the case involved Catholics and the district court was located in New York, the percentage of Catholics in New York in 1990 was (hypothetically) 44.3%; hence, this is the measure which would be entered. In this way one hopes to estimate the extent to which activist federal court judges in these cases were responsive to the preferences of various religious affiliations within their states. And, of course, whether there is a marked difference between activist and non-activist judges in this regard. Information on the religious compositions within states was gathered from Kosmin and Lachman (1993).

Since the dependent variable is dichotomous (whether the judge is an activist) and there are multiple independent variables, statistical analysis will involve the use of probit. Probit analysis has been employed is similar research contexts. (Segal 1984; Wenner and Dutter 1988, Yarnold 1990a, 1991a.)

FINDINGS

Table I shows the results of probit analysis. The initial data set included 663 cases, 326 cases were rejected due to missing data, and 337 cases remain.

None of the variables are statistically significant.

Judges who were activists were more likely than the non-activists to render a decision that was anti-partisan, hence, for example, a Republican judge would enter an anti-religion decision, but this was not significant. Activist judges were also more likely than the non-activists to render decisions that awarded losses to pro-religion groups, but again, this is not significant. Though also not significant, activist judges were also somewhat more likely than the non-activist to award "wins" to the anti-religion groups. Further, activists were more than the non-activists to respond in their decisions to the religious composition of their state, as reflected in the various religions that arose in the cases, though this variable was not significant.

DISCUSSION

A few possibilities emerge in terms of interpreting these results. First, it may be argued that since there was so little variance in the dependant measure, namely, whether district court judges are political activists, since an overwhelming majority of these judges were activists prior to their appointment, what we see, in fact, is that both activists and non-activists render similar decisions in cases involving religious liberties since they are confronted by the same political and environmental forces in their highly politicized judicial environment.

Similarly, given their lifetime of immersion in partisan politics, it is not at all surprising that activist judges, or judges who had held either elective or appointive office prior to their appointment to the federal bench, did not display any major patterns that would distinguish them in any significant way from the non-activist judges. They have crafted well their survival skills in the volatile world of politics and carry these skills with mastery to their new positions in the federal courts. Hence, not surprisingly, the activists tended to distance themselves from their parties, but would not completely sever the relationship. Hence, the activists were inclined to rule against their party's position in the religious freedoms cases, but in a most anemic manner. Afterall, if they contemplate further advances within or outside of the federal judiciary, it is useful to have the home party to call upon when it can render further service.

Similarly, the activist judges, aware of the need to maintain positive relationships with interest groups, did a balancing act between the pro- and the anti-religion groups which became involved in the religious liberties litigation. The activists were slightly more likely to rule against the pro-religion groups than the non-activists, but this negative vote was so slight as to be almost nonexistent, ensuring no backlash from politically powerful groups within the pro-religion lobby. The activists were instead, slightly more likely than the non-activists to render decisions which favored the anti-religion groups, including civil liberties groups, but the support was seemingly lackluster and again, very weak. The groups which appeared in these cases, including, for example, religious organizations and civil liberties groups, are potent actors in judicial appointments, and hence the activist judges carefully split their decisions between the various pro- and anti-religion groups.

Finally, with respect to the judicial constituency measure, the activists were slightly more likely than the non-activists to render decisions that favored state-based religions which appeared in the cases. In short, if the case involved a religion which was well-represented in the judge's home state, then the activist judges were more likely than the non-activists to render a decision that favored that particular religion. But, the activist judges also did not want to appear parochial and beholden to local religious interests, and hence, this support was very weak.

Hence, a general pattern which emerges is that activist judges in the religious liberties cases evaluated here gave ample evidence of their political survival skills. They skillfully maneuvered in these cases so that they were not seemingly captured by any political force, including their parties, pro and anti-religion groups, and by their judicial constituents--in the religious liberties cases, the religious composition of their states and the extent to which these religions were represented in cases before them.

Table 1
Probit Estimates for Activist District Court Judges In Religious Liberties Cases, 1970-1990
Dependent Variable: Is Judge An Activist?

Variable	Maximum Likelihood Error (MLE)	Standard Estimate (S.E.)	MLE/S.E.
Constant	5.78	.13	43.66
Partisan Decision	-.09	.15	-.58
Pro-Religion Groups	-.03	.18	-.17
Anti-Religion Groups	.02	.24	.09
Religious Constituency	.01	.01	.85

Chi-Square = 336.58 DF = 332 P = .42 N = 337
* Significant at .05.

Chapter 3

DID DISTRICT JUDGES OVERCOME THEIR OWN RELIGIONS IN RELIGIOUS LIBERTIES CASES?

The research examines whether the outcome in these cases (defined as a pro-religion decision) is related to the judges' religious affiliations (or lack of religious faith), and whether litigants were helped by the fact that they shared the same religions as the judges who adjudicated the cases. The religious affiliations which are included in the analysis are as follows: Methodist, Presbyterian, Baptist, Episcopalian, Catholic, Lutheran, Jewish, and non-religious.

DATA AND METHODS

The same data is used as utilized in Chapter 4.

The dependent variable is: is the decision beneficial to religion (a dichotomous dependent variable)? Information on judges' religious affiliations, or the fact that they are non-religious, is gathered from Judicial Staff Directory (Brownson 1991), and from another source book, The American Bench (Lichterman 1978).

FINDINGS

Table 2 shows the results of probit analysis. The initial data set included 624 cases, 42 cases were rejected due to missing data, and 582 cases remain.

Two of the variables are statistically significant: the fact that judges are Jewish and that they are Baptist. Judges who were identified as Jewish were significantly more likely to decide a case involving religious liberties in a pro-religion manner than the other judges. Baptist judges, on the other hand, were, at a statistically significant level, more likely to enter a decision that was anti-religion. Although not significant, Lutheran and Presbyterian judges were also more likely than the other judges to favor religion. Interestingly, some denominations were associated with an anti-religion stance. The highest anti-religion record was for Baptist judges followed, in descending order, by Episcopalian, Methodist, and Catholic judges. Judges who were non-religious were slightly more likely than other judges to decide cases in an anti-religion manner, but this was not significant.

Judges who were of the same religion as those involved in the litigation were only slightly more likely to render a decision in their favor.

DISCUSSION

Consistent with the norm of “liberal” Jewish judges, religious Jewish judges were more likely to render a decision that was pro-religion in cases involving religious liberties than were other judges. Perhaps due to the fact that they have traditionally been a minority religious denomination in the U.S., it may be that Jewish judges who were practicing their faith were more receptive to the claims of other religious minorities, who filed their First Amendment claims with the federal courts. Next in line in terms of their support for religious liberties were Presbyterian and Lutheran judges, who were also more likely than other judges to decide religious liberties cases in a pro-religion manner.

Not all religious denominations followed the pro-religion lead, however. Judges who were Baptist were more likely to enter decisions that were anti-religion, followed, in descending order, by Episcopalian, Methodist, and Catholic judges.

The only significant anti-religion variable, though was recorded for the Baptist judges. Judges who were Baptist were significantly more likely than others to render an anti-religion decision. In contrast to the Jewish judges, who showed some level of tolerance for all religions, the same cannot be said for the Baptist judges. Perhaps it is due to the fact that fact that the Baptist religion is extremely doctrinaire, indicating that the only way to salvation is through being a member of this religion.

Hence, most of the judges did, in fact overcome their own religious predilections in these cases, with the only exception of Jewish and Baptist judges. But even when the variables did not reach statistical significance, patterns emerge which suggest that judges affiliated with religions which have endured minority status (Jews) tend to be more supportive of religious liberties claims in the federal courts than judges affiliated with mainline Protestant denominations. However, judges did not, at significant level, favor members of their own religions in these cases.

In a country which has traditionally been the home to those fleeing religious persecution, it is arguably appropriate that the judges of the U.S. district courts reflected a plurality of religions and religious philosophies which were, ultimately, reflected in the decisions in these cases.

To those who tend to be more concerned with free exercise by this country's many religions, this outcome may be perfectly appropriate. To the extent that pluralism may be achieved in the world of judicial politics, it is appropriate that different religious philosophies had their say on questions of the greatest concern to them: religious liberties.

To those who are more concerned with the non-establishment mandate of the First Amendment, these results may be troubling. The objective federal bench was seemingly pulled by the various religious philosophies of its constituent judges, and thus absconded its responsibility of ensuring that a "wall of separation" exists between state and religion. Indeed, the wall is exposed as nothing but a veneer or convenient judicial metaphor which masks, as always, a highly amorphous institution with enormous power and discretion.

Table 1
Probit Estimates for District Court Judges' Religious Affiliations In Religious Liberties Cases, 1979-1990
Dependent Variable: Decision Was Pro-Religion

Variable	Maximum Likelihood Error(MLE)	Standard Estimate (S.E.)	MLE/S.E.
Constant	4.96	.17	29.78
Is Judge Non-Religious?	-.11	.18	-.61
Same Religion?	.19	.28	.68
Methodist	-.12	.25	-.47
Presbyterian	.04	.25	.16
Baptist	-.99	.38	-2.58*
Episcopalian	-.21	.24	-.87
Catholic	-.02	.21	-.12
Lutheran	.04	.40	.10
Jewish	.55	.29	1.89*

Chi-Square = 582.16 DF = 572 P = .38
N = 394
* Significant at .05.

Chapter 4

FACTORS RELATED TO OUTCOMES IN RELIGIOUS FREEDOMS CASES, FEDERAL DISTRICT COURTS: 1970-1990

This project evaluates, for the period of 1970-1990, decision making by the federal courts in cases which concern religious liberties, protected by the First Amendment of the U.S. Constitution. Specifically, for these two decades, the analysis concentrates on federal court cases which deal with the free exercise and establishment clauses of the First Amendment. The research is at the district court level. Yarnold (1992, N.d.) has argued in previous research that political variables (including the partisanship of judges, the presumed desires of "judicial constituents" and the involvement of interest groups in litigation) may be significantly related to judicial decision making when the issue is a "major" issue and/or when powerful groups are interested in the outcome of the case. Since cases involving religious freedoms are major, controversial, and well-publicized cases, this analysis will serve as a good test of the organizing framework for politicized judicial decision making. Similarly, it was hypothesized that region might be significantly related to judicial outcomes when the issue considered by the courts is one with high ideological content (Yarnold 1992, 1995, N.d.). Once again, the religious freedoms cases will serve as a good test of this proposition.

In addition to examining the partisanship of judges, interest group involvement, and judicial constituents, it also divides judges into either activist judges (on the basis of their prior political and administrative positions) or non-activist and attempts to assess whether political activism is related to a more supportive posture toward religious freedom. In addition to improving the political analysis of court cases, the research will include as control variables whether the outcome in these cases is related to the judges' religious affiliations (or lack of religious faith), the ages of the judges, and their gender.

RELIGIOUS FREEDOMS AND THE FEDERAL COURTS

Unlike the other "fundamental" rights contained in the First Amendment to the U.S. Constitution, including freedom of speech, press and assembly, which are arguably necessary to the functioning of a representative democracy on the basis that they serve to provide for a more enlightened and informed electorate, the free exercise and establishment clauses of the same amendment are fundamental not due to political necessity but due to historical accident: the fact that so many of the colonists had fled religious persecution in other countries. This is not meant to imply that the religious freedoms clauses of the First Amendment are secondary in any way to the others, it is instead to suggest the vital importance of religious liberty in our constitutional schema, grounded as it is in our nation's history, customs, and political culture.

Although immigrants to the United States may have often been united in their search for religious freedom, it has also been the case that religious differences in this country have led to division.

Religious groups were often segregated economically, politically, socially, and even geographically (Kosmin and Lachman 1993). Underlying the debate were fundamental questions which were to guide men and women to truth, morality, justice, and knowledge of their creator. Each religious group unfortunately, tended to answer these fundamental questions with highly or slightly idiosyncratic principles. As a result, debates within the religious community were often filled with friction. To make matters worse, also entering the debate were those who insisted that they had no religious belief and did not want the state to proselytize them in any manner.

The federal courts were given the task of making order out of this disorder, through their presumably apolitical and objective interpretation of the free exercise and establishment clauses of the First Amendment. Needless to say, their interpretations of the religious freedoms clauses in specific cases has engendered even more debate, within the legal community, among legal scholars, among the press, policy makers, and the general public. Not surprisingly, there are many critics. And the criticism seems to be warranted at times, when after reviewing cases in perhaps a course on constitutional law, one finds that the rules which emanate from the federal courts in cases dealing with religious freedoms seem to change, are often unclear, conflicting, and impossible to reconcile. A frantic law student studying for a test may surmise unhappily, "perhaps there are no rules."

Although the legal community has been quite thorough in its doctrinal analysis of court cases involving religious liberties (Tribe 1988, Gey 1990, Laycock 1991, Brown 1993, Choper 1995), the same cannot be said of the public law area. To date, relatively few public law analyses of cases involving the free exercise and establishment clauses of the First Amendment have been conducted. Another general observation is that much of the research in the public law area has focused upon the U.S. Supreme Court, and not on the lower federal courts (Shapiro 1993). For these reasons, the proposed research is not likely to be redundant.

The research will utilize for its purposes federal district court cases which deal with the free exercise and establishment clauses. There are several reasons for dealing with both clauses simultaneously. The first is pragmatic: most judicial decisions which deal with religious liberties discuss both clauses. Second, from a more theoretical perspective, the free exercise and establishment clauses share a common purpose, namely protecting the liberties of religious individuals and the non-religious. Finally, it is based upon an underlying skepticism about the importance of rules, and even the existence of rules, concepts which have emerged in the public law area.

HYPOTHESES

The project draws upon Yarnold's prior work in the public law area, which has been concerned with the question of why federal court outcomes are related to political factors (including interest group involvement in litigation, the partisanship of judges, and the preferences of judicial constituencies), and to the environment, while in other types of cases political factors do not reach the level of statistical significance (Yarnold 1990a, 1990b, 1991, 1992, 1994a, 1994b, 1995a, 1195b, N.d.). Drawing upon this research and that of others, an organizing framework was developed (Yarnold 1992, N.d.) which predicts that federal courts, in spite of lifetime appointments, are likely to respond to political factors when the case in question involves a "major issue," defined as an issue that is regularly reported by the media, receives public scrutiny, and tends to conform with divisions between the Democratic and Republican parties. This, incidentally, is an adaptation of Page et. al's (1983) earlier work on congressional decision making. Hence, in Yarnold's previous research, in asylum and refugee appeals from 1980-1987 and abortion cases adjudicated during the period 1973-1990, both dealing with major issues, the outcomes were related to political factors.

In contrast, in cases dealing with international extradition, judicial outcomes were not related to the same political factors (interest group involvement, judicial constituents, and partisanship). Although these types of cases are of immense interest to certain ethnic groups in the United States, they are not well-publicized and not likely to divide the electorate along partisan lines. Hence, international extradition is not, arguably, a major issue. However, it was observed that the individuals who were subject to extradition requests were much more likely to prevail if they were linked to the IRA, while those linked to the PLO were much less likely to prevail. It was argued that the Irish lobby in the U.S. is much stronger than the Palestinian lobby. Hence, a second part of the model predicts that other cases in which judicial outcomes may be related to political factors are those which involve non-major issues, but are nevertheless of interest to major groups in the U.S.

In most of Yarnold's research, region was also included in the analysis. However, in asylum and international extradition cases, region was not significant. In contrast, in many analyses region has been found to be significantly related to judicial outcomes, for example, in environmental litigation (Wenner 1982; Wenner and Dutter 1988) and race relations cases (Richardson and Vines 1978). To reconcile these disparate findings, Yarnold (1995) suggested that region might be most likely to be significant in cases which deal with a highly ideological issue, such as abortion. Hence, in fact, in abortion cases, region was found to be significantly related to the outcome (Yarnold 1995a, 1995b).

One of the major research objectives of this study is to test, in the context of religious liberty cases (or cases which involve the free exercise or establishment clauses), clearly cases which involve major issues, the various predictions of the organizing framework for politized judicial decisions. Specifically, are outcomes in these cases related to "political factors" (the involvement of interest groups in litigation, judicial constituents, and the partisanship of judges)? Further, since these cases are also highly ideological, are the outcomes significantly related to region? Of course, if the predictions are unsupported by the analysis, the hope is then to fashion a new or modified one in light of the findings.

It is also anticipated that the power of the model will be enhanced by the addition of the "political activism" inquiry. In other words, it is anticipated that judges who were political activists prior to their ascent to the federal bench (they held political and/or appointive office), will decide the religious freedoms cases differently from those who were not political activists.

In addition to improving the political analysis of court cases, the research will also examine other facets of the judicial environment which may also help to understand decisions in cases involving religious liberties. The dependent variable is whether the judicial decision is one which is pro-religion. The additional control variables which will be included relate to arguably relevant factors relating to the judges including: their religious affiliations (or lack of religious belief), their ages, and their gender.

DATA AND METHODS

A couple of sample cases will help to introduce the data set employed in this analysis of religious freedoms cases.

In Dawson v. Mizell, 325 F.Supp. 511 (Ed. Va. 1971), a post office worker claimed that the employer, the U.S. post office, had violated the employee's free exercise rights since the employee was a 7th Day Adventist and, in violation of the tenets of that faith, was forced to work on Saturdays (the Sabbath). The case was presided over by the Honorable Robert R. Merhige, who had been appointed by Johnson in 1967, was a Catholic, had not been a political activist, and was a member of the Democratic Party. The case had no interest group involvement and was presided over by a male judge who was 52 years of age at the time that the decision was rendered. The case was decided by a court in the South, in Richmond, Virginia which had a low percentage of 7th Day Adventists in the state; only .4% of the state's population were 7th Day Adventists. The decision went against the plaintiff, the court holding that there had been no violation of the free exercise rights of the 7th Day Adventist as a result of the U.S. Post Office's requiring the plaintiff to work on the Sabbath. In this case, the decision was coded anti-religion since it did not serve to advance the ability of the plaintiff to practice his or her faith.

The case of the Gilfillan v. City of Philadelphia, 480 F.Supp. 1161 (E.D. Pa., 1979), involved a taxpayer suit against the City of Philadelphia, based on the First Amendment, which sought an injunction against that city's use of public funds to construct a base that was to be used for a Papal Mass. The religion which was involved in the case was the Roman Catholic religion and the case arose in Philadelphia, Pennsylvania, in the Northeast. The plaintiff was assisted by two groups in this case, the American Civil Liberties Union and by National Ministries, American Baptist Churches in the United States of America. The presiding judge was Raymond J. Broderick who had been appointed by President Nixon in 1971, and was a Republican. The judge was a Catholic, a male, a political activist, and 65 at the time that the decision was rendered. The court found for the plaintiff, holding that the use of public funds for a Papal Mass would violate the First Amendment. Over a third (33%) of Pennsylvania's population was Catholic. The decision was coded as anti-religion once again, because it did serve to promote the free exercise rights of Roman Catholics, for whom a Papal Mass is an important religious occasion.

Official Reporters (the **Federal Supplement**) were used to gather cases for this analysis. The cases included here are for two decades, from 1970-1990. The total data set is 667 district court cases decided during this period. The dependent variable in the public law analysis of court cases is: is the decision beneficial to religion (a dichotomous dependent variable)? Specifically, cases usually involved one or more religious denomination and if the decision benefited the specific denomination, then the decision was coded as "pro-religion." There was no attempt to evaluate whether the decision benefited religion in a more holistic or general sense since this would lead to great difficulty in coding the dependent variable, and lend itself to inappropriate subjective "guesses" about the extent to which religion in general was benefited by a particular judicial outcome. The more conservative approach adopted here--namely limiting the analysis to whether religious individuals and organizations who were litigants in these cases prevailed--has advantages in terms of conceptual clarity and limiting the scope of the inquiry. This conservative approach, however, also had disadvantages, since a number of cases had to be excluded from the analysis as they made no specific mention of a particular religious organization.

Information on interest group involvement in the cases will be derived from reading the cases, which typically list the interest groups. Information on the partisan affiliation of judges, their religions (or lack of religious affiliation), their ages, and their gender will be gathered from a **Judicial Staff Directory** (Brownson 1991), and from another source book, **The American Bench** (Lichterman 1978). These sources will also be used to determine whether the judges are political activists, with judges gaining this designation if, in their pre-appointment activities, they held one or more elective or appointive office. Wenner's (1982; 1988) typology of region will be used for coding the region variable in this analysis. The "judicial constituency" variable in these cases is measured as follows: the case will be scanned to determine which religion is in issue. For example, a case involving a use of public funds for a Papal Mass will be coded: Roman Catholic. Most of the cases are much more straightforward, however, involving an individual who is either filing an action or defending an action and indicates his or her religious affiliation. In other instances, as where an ordinance allows for the maintenance of a lighted cross in a public park, there is usually no specific religion involved but it will fall into the category of "general Christian." In these cases, there has been no attempt to categorize the religion. After ascertaining the religion in dispute, such as Roman Catholic, the state in which the case was adjudicated is identified. From this, the judicial constituency variable is measured as: percentage of the state population which is the religion in question. Hence if the home state of the case were Rhode Island, and the case involved Roman Catholics, a measure is made of the percentage of the population in Rhode Island in 1990 that was Catholic: 61.7% The information on the religious populations within states is derived from *Religion in Contemporary American Society*, by Kosmin and Lachman (Crown Publishers, Inc. 1993). Once again, as in the case of the dependent variable, if there is no specific mention in the case of a religious denomination, the case is excluded from the analysis.

Since the dependent variable is dichotomous (whether the outcome is pro-religion) and there are multiple independent variables, statistical analysis will involve the use of probit. Probit analysis has been employed is similar research contexts. (Segal 1984; Wenner and Dutter 1988, Yarnold 1990a, 1991a.)

The measurement of the independent variables is as follows: the age of the judge at the time he or she rendered a decision, is the judge male, is the judge religious, is the judge a political activist, is the judge a member of the Republican Party, are there pro-religion interest groups involved in the case, are there anti-religion interest groups in the case, what is the percentage in 1990 of the judge's state that is of the same religion that appears in the case, is the case presided over by federal district courts in the South, the Midwest, the Northeast, or the West?

FINDINGS

Table 1
Probit Estimates for Federal District Court Religious Liberties Cases, 1970-1990
Dependent Variable: Decision Was Pro-Religion

Variable	Maximum Likelihood Error(MLE)	Standard Estimate (S.E.)	MLE/S.E.
Constant	4.95	.65	7.60
Is Judge Religious?	.06	.15	.39
Age of Judges	- .01	.01	- .91
Is Judge Male?	.89	.32	2.83 *
Is Judge a Republican?	- .17	.15	- 1.12
Is Judge an Activist?	.02	.17	.12
Are There Pro-Religion Groups?	.27	.14	1.84 *
Are There Anti-Religion Groups?	- .08	.18	- .44
% Judge's State Population 1990 Same Religion As in Case	- .01	.01	- 1.34
South	- .45	.25	- 1.81 *
Midwest	- .66	.24	- 2.75 *
Northeast	- .35	.23	- 1.52

Chi-Square = 326.4 DF = 316 P = .33
N = 328
* Significant at .05.

Table I shows the results of probit analysis. One deficiency with probit is that it deletes cases that have missing data, and in this analysis, missing data occurred primarily in connection with three variables: the dependent variable, namely whether the decision benefited the particular religion(s) involved in the case, and two independent variables: the religion involved in the case (for the purpose of the "judicial constituency" measure) and the religious affiliations of the judges. The first two problems arose simply because the opinions filed by judges did not mention a religion. The third deficiency arose because judges are reluctant to provide their religious affiliations to judicial biographers. These problems, are however, unavoidable. Hence, though the initial data set included 667 cases, 339 cases were rejected due to missing data, and 328 cases remain. There is no reason to suspect any systematic bias in the data as a result of the deletion of cases, since they were not deliberate and occurred due to chance. Hence, the remaining cases are likely representative of the total population of cases.

There are four statistically significant variables: the fact that judges are male, that there are pro-religion interest groups involved in the litigation, that the case was decided in the Midwest, and in the South.

DISCUSSION

The main prediction of the general theory of public law is that in federal court cases that involve major, publicized issues, political factors will be related to the outcome. What one observes is that in cases dealing with religious liberties, the involvement of pro-religion groups in litigation--a political factor--is significantly related to the outcome in these cases. More specifically, the involvement of pro-religion groups in litigation was significantly related to a pro-religion decision by the federal courts in cases dealing with the free exercise and establishment clauses of the First Amendment. Hence, the most important hypothesis of the general model is supported (or not rejected) in the analysis.

The political activism, measure, however, does not add to our understanding of the political dynamics of the federal judiciary. Federal judges who were classified as political activists due to the fact that they held one or more elective and/or appointive office prior to their ascension to the federal bench were slightly more likely to render a pro-religion decision, but this variable is not significant.

Other political factors which were not significantly related to a pro-religion outcome in these cases relate to the partisanship of the federal judges and their judicial constituencies. Although Republican judges were less likely than Democratic judges to render a pro-religion decision, this variable was not significant. As the percentage of a state's population increased relative to the religion at issue in a case, the higher the probability that the court would issue an anti-religion decision. In short, the federal courts were not, in these cases, responsive to the fact that the religions which arose in these cases were well-represented in the judges' states.

Another political factor which was not significantly related to the outcomes in these cases was the involvement of anti-religion groups.

Two of the regional variables were significantly related to the outcomes in these cases. Courts in the West were the only courts which tended to have pro-religion outcomes, but this was not significant. All other regions recorded ant-religion outcomes, including the Northeast (not significant), the South (significant), and the Midwest (significant).

Federal judges who indicated that they were religious were slightly more likely to render a pro-religion decision than others, but this variable is not significant. As the ages of the judges increased, they were less likely to render a pro-religion decision.

Also interesting is the fact that male judges were significantly more likely to render a pro-religion decision than female judges. Hence, an apparent gender difference arises in these cases. Further research is called for to evaluate why this gender difference might arise. One possibility is that most of the female judges tend to be relatively new additions to the federal bench. Perhaps they are just beginning their acculturation or assimilation into the lower federal bench and once this process is complete, they will resemble more in their decision making their male counterparts on the bench.

With regard to the split finding with regard to the significance of interest groups in federal court litigation, with pro-religion groups in religious liberties being significant players as compared to the anti-religion groups, these split findings were replicated in an earlier analysis of abortion cases (Yarnold 1995a, 1995b). In the abortion cases, the involvement of pro-choice groups in litigation was significantly related to pro-choice court decisions, while involvement by the pro-life groups was not significantly related to the outcome.

In an attempt to reconcile these findings, organizations which were involved in abortion litigation were surveyed (Yarnold 1995a, 1995b). The objective was to determine whether the organizations' success in litigation was related to the political resources of the groups or to their litigation resources/"repeat player" status. The analysis suggested that, when controlling for the litigation resources and political resources of the groups, the only factor which was significantly related to successful judicial outcomes was a political one: namely, the identity of the group. Specifically, civil liberties groups and Planned Parenthood were both, at a level of statistical significance, successful organizational players in abortion cases. It was posited that the courts were unwilling to rule against such politically powerful players in judicial politics.

By the same token, it may be that the federal court judges in the religious liberties cases, in favoring pro-religion groups and not anti-religion groups, were responding to the same stimuli. Further research is indicated along these lines.

To those who tend to be more concerned with free exercise by this country's many religions, this outcome may be perfectly appropriate. To the extent that pluralism may be achieved in the world of judicial politics, it is appropriate that religious organizations and other pro-religion groups had their say on questions of the greatest concern to them: religious liberties. Of course, this presumes that broad representation of all religious interests was achieved. It cannot be ascertained at this point if this, in fact, occurred. Certainly, further research will be conducted to further examine this important issue.

To those who are more concerned with the non-establishment mandate, these results will indeed be troubling. The apolitical federal courts responded to the weight of the organized pro-religion forces in these cases, and thus absconded their responsibility to ensure that a "wall of separation" exists between state and religion. Indeed, the wall is exposed as nothing but a veneer or convenient judicial metaphor which masks, as always, a highly political institution with enormous policy making authority.

Chapter 5

VIEWING THE "INNER CIRCLE": CIRCUIT COURTS OF APPEALS JUDGES IN RELIGIOUS FREEDOMS CASES, 1970-1990

This book focuses upon federal court decisions which deal with religious liberties, namely either the free exercise or non-establishment clause of the 1st Amendment to the U.S. Constitution. The time span involved is two decades, from 1970-1990. This section focuses upon the circuit courts of appeals.

Perhaps the greatest insight into the politicized nature of the federal courts have been offered by Baum (1989). In his work on the lower federal courts and the U.S. Supreme Court, he points out that these courts are immersed in politics in spite of the fact that they are presumably shielded from these influences due to their lifetime appointments.

However, Baum (1989) notes that these judges have, for the most part, been selected based upon their prior work for political parties, and that almost all of the judges are of the same political party as their appointing Presidents. He went on to analyze characteristics of typical federal judges and found that most of these judges have held political and/or appointive office prior to their selection to the federal judiciary.

In this twenty-year survey of federal circuit court of appeals judges involved in religious freedoms cases, the same observations hold. Namely, federal court judges had often, for example served as state court judges, served either in state legislatures or in Congress, or served as the Attorney Generals for their states. Further, this politicized activity was the rule rather than the exception. This study classified district court judges as a "political activists" if they had held one or more political or appointive office prior to their appointment. Eighty-percent (80%) of the judges were found to be political activists. Those who were not activists were often private attorneys with distinguished records, many of whom had held positions on bar organizations external to mainstream U.S. politics. Hence, they were legal activists rather than political activists. There was the occasional law professor who was also appointed who was not a political activist.

Given the fact that most of these judges had long careers in partisan politics prior to their appointment to the federal bench, it is not surprising that they are not a particularly young group. For the federal circuit court of appeals judges that adjudicated religious freedoms cases during the period 1970-1990, the average age was 61 years of age.

In spite of the fact that in recent years, women roughly equal men in numbers in terms of admissions to law schools, in the religious freedoms cases surveyed here, 99% of the judges were men, while only 1% were women. On the other hand, the judges were evenly split in terms of their partisanship, with 47% of the judges being members of the Democratic Party, while 53% were Republicans.

Given the salience of these issues to major organized religious groups, it is not surprising there was heavy involvement in these cases of pro-religion interest groups, or groups who supported the 1st

Amendment rights of a particular religion. Forty-one percent of these cases involved pro-religion groups. The pro-religion groups included not only religious organizations, but other actors, such as civil liberties groups. Since some of these cases involved indigent prisoners who claimed their religious rights had been violated by prison officials, legal aid groups often also made their appearance, as well as ad-hoc citizens groups which argued that, for example, the public schools were violating the religious freedoms of their students.

Nineteen percent of the religious freedoms cases also involved anti-religion groups, and these included, for example, civil liberties groups, organizations committed to preventing the intermixture of religion with public institutions, labor unions which argued that workers should be forced to pay union dues and/or join unions in spite of the fact that their religions proscribed such activities, and teacher's unions that battled to ensure that funds allocated to public schools should be restricted to public schools and not expended on religious schools.

The religion cases occurred most often in the Midwest (32% of the cases) and the South (21% of the cases). Both Western states and States in the North were each included in 20% of the cases, while only 6% of the cases were adjudicated in D.C.

In terms of the religious backgrounds of the judges, 70% indicated that they belong to a religious denomination, leaving about 30% non-religious.

Chapter 6

Did Activist Circuit Courts of Appeals Judges Decide Cases Involving Religious Liberties Differently than Non-Activist Judges? 1970-1990

This project evaluates, for the period of 1970-1990, decision making by the federal courts in cases which concern religious liberties, protected by the First Amendment of the U.S. Constitution. Specifically, the analysis concentrates on federal court cases which deal with the free exercise and establishment clauses of the First Amendment.

The research is at the circuit courts of appeals level, and examines whether activist judges were more likely than non-activist judges to render decisions in these cases that were responsive to the partisanship of the judges, the participation of both pro- and anti-religion groups, and the judicial constituencies which are represented in these cases.

RELIGIOUS FREEDOMS AND THE FEDERAL COURTS

Unlike the other "fundamental" rights contained in the First Amendment to the U.S. Constitution, including freedom of speech, press and assembly, which are arguably necessary to the functioning of a representative democracy, the free exercise and establishment clauses of the same amendment are fundamental not due to political necessity but due to historical accident: the fact that so many of the colonists had fled religious persecution in other countries. This is not meant to imply that the religious freedoms clauses of the First Amendment are secondary in any way to the others, it is instead to suggest the vital importance of religious liberty in our constitutional schema, grounded as it is in our nation's history, customs, and political culture.

Although immigrants to the United States may have often been united in their search for religious freedom, it has also been the case that religious differences in this country have led to division. Religious groups were often segregated economically, politically, socially, and even geographically (Kosmin and Lachman 1993). Underlying the debate were fundamental questions which were to guide men and women to truth, morality, justice, and knowledge of their creator. Each religious group unfortunately, tended to answer these fundamental questions with highly or slightly idiosyncratic principles. As a result, debates within the religious community were often filled with friction. To make matters worse, also entering the debate were those who insisted that they had no religious belief and did not want the state to proselytize them in any manner.

The federal courts were given the task of making order out of this disorder, through their apolitical, objective, and almost scientific interpretation of the free exercise and establishment clauses of the First Amendment. Needless to say, their interpretations of the religious freedoms clauses in specific cases has engendered even more debate, within the legal community, among legal scholars,

among the press, policy makers, and the general public. Not surprisingly, there are many critics. And the criticism seems to be warranted at times, when after reviewing cases in perhaps a course on constitutional law, one finds that the rules which emanate from the federal courts in cases dealing with religious freedoms seem to change, are often unclear, conflicting, and impossible to reconcile. A frantic law student studying for a test may surmise unhappily, "perhaps there are no rules."

Although the legal community has been quite thorough in its doctrinal analysis of court cases involving religious liberties (Tribe 1988, Gey 1990, Laycock 1991, Brown 1993, Choper 1995), the same cannot be said of the public law area. To date, relatively few public law analyses of cases involving the free exercise and establishment clauses of the First Amendment have been conducted. Another general observation is that much of the research in the public law area has focused upon the U.S. Supreme Court, and not on the lower federal courts (Shapiro 1993). There have been few, if any, similar analyses of whether activist federal circuit courts of appeals judges are more or less responsive in their decision making than non-activist judges to their partisan affiliations, the involvement of pro-and anti-religion groups, and the presumed desires of their judicial constituents. For these reasons, the proposed research is not likely to be redundant.

The research utilizes for its purposes federal circuit courts of appeals cases which deal with the free exercise and establishment clauses.

DATA AND METHODS

Official Reporters (Federal Reporters) were used to gather cases for this analysis. The cases included here are for two decades, from 1970 to 1990. The total data set is 404 circuit courts of appeals cases decided during this period. The dependent variable is: is the judge an activist (a dichotomous dependent variable)? Information on judicial activism is gathered from Judicial Staff Directory (Brownson, 1991) and from another source book, The American Bench (Lichterman 1978). Judges were deemed to be activists if they held one or more political and/or appointive offices prior to their appointment to the federal bench. Since the courts here consist of panels of three judges, the panel is categorized as being comprised of activist judges if two of more of the judges are political activists.

The independent variables relating to partisanship, pro-religion interest group litigation, anti-religion interest group litigation, and the preferences of judicial constituents, were coded in the following manner. The judge was deemed to have responded to his or her party ties if he or she were a Republican judge and decided the case in a pro-religion manner, and if he or she were a Democratic judge and decided the case in an anti-religion manner.

Once again, since were are dealing with panels of three judges as decision makers, the panels were categorized as "Republican" panels if two or more judges on the court were Republicans, and alternately, as "Democratic" judges if two or more of the appeals judges were members of the Democratic Party.

For the pro-interest group measure, judges were deemed to have entered a pro-religious group decision in a case if the pro-religion group won the case (and a pro-religion decision was entered). Anti-religious groups were also recorded as being successful litigants if they won their case (and thus an anti-religion decision was entered). To compute the judicial constituency measure, for each case, a measure was taken of the religious affiliations that were involved in the case, for example, Mormons. Since each judge resides within a particular state, a measure was taken of the percentage of that state's population which shares the same religion as the one involved in the case. For example, if the case involved Catholics and the appeals court was located in New York, the percentage of Catholics in New

York in 1990 was (hypothetically) 44.3%. Since again we are dealing with three judges, they may all reside within one state, two states, or three different states. A measure is taken for all three states of the religious composition measure (for "Roman Catholics, for example) and from this, a mean score for all three states is computed.

In this way one hopes to estimate the extent to which activist federal court judges in these cases were responsive to the preferences of various religious affiliations within their states. And, of course, whether there is a marked difference between activist and non-activist judges in this regard. Information on the religious compositions within states was gathered from Kosmin and Lachman (1993).

Since the dependent variable is dichotomous (whether the judge is an activist) and there are multiple independent variables, statistical analysis will involve the use of probit. Probit analysis has been employed is similar research contexts. (Segal 1984; Wenner and Dutter 1988, Yarnold 1990a, 1991a.)

FINDINGS

Table I shows the results of probit analysis. The initial data set included 404 cases, 155 of the cases were rejected due to missing data, and 249 cases remain.

One of the variables is statistically significant.

Judges who were activists were more likely than the non-activists to render a decision that was pro-partisan, hence, for example, a Republican judge would enter an pro-religion decision, but this was not significant. Activist judges were also more likely than the non-activists to award wins to pro-religion groups, but again, this is not significant. Though also not significant, activist judges were also somewhat more likely than the non-activists to award "losses" to the anti-religion groups.

The only variable which is statistically significant is the judicial constituency measure in these cases. Judges who were activists were more likely than the non-activists to respond positively to the fact that the religions which appeared in the cases were well-represented in terms of total state populations, within the judges' states.

Table 1
Probit Estimates for Activist Circuit Courts Of Appeals Judges In Religious Liberties Cases, 1970-1990
Dependent Variable: Is Judge An Activist?

Variable	Maximum Likelihood Error (MLE)	Standard Estimate (S.E.)	MLE/S.E.
Constant	5.69	.14 39	.36
Partisan Decision	.18	.19	.96
Pro-Religion Groups	.10	.25	.40
Anti-Religion Groups	-.06	.13	-.45
Religious Constituency	.01	.00	1.67*

Chi-Square = 248.33 DF = 244 P = .41
N = 249
* Significant at .05.

DISCUSSION

Given their lifetime of immersion in partisan politics, it is not at all surprising that activist judges, or judges who had held either elective or appointive office prior to the federal bench, did not display any major patterns that would distinguish them in any significant way from the non-activist judges. They have crafted well their survival skills in the volatile world of politics and carry these skills with mastery to their new positions in the federal courts. Hence, not surprisingly, the activists tended to distance themselves from their parties, but would not completely sever the relationship. Hence, the activists were inclined to rule in favor of their party's position in the religious freedoms cases, but in a most anemic manner. After all, if they contemplate further advances within or outside of the federal judiciary, it is useful to have the home party to call upon when it can render further service.

Similarly, the activist judges, aware of the need to maintain positive relationships with interest groups, did a balancing act between the pro- and the anti-religion groups which became involved in the religious liberties litigation. The activists were slightly more likely to rule in favor of the pro-religion groups than the non-activists, but this support was so slight as to be almost nonexistent, ensuring no backlash from politically powerful groups within the anti-religion lobby. The activists were instead, slightly more likely than the non-activists to render losses to the anti-religion groups, including civil liberties groups, but the support was seemingly lackluster and again, very weak. The groups which appeared in these cases, including, for example, religious organizations and civil liberties groups, are potent actors in judicial appointments, and hence the activist judges carefully split their decisions between the various pro- and anti-religion groups.

Finally, with respect to the judicial constituency measure, the activists were significantly more likely than the non-activists to render decisions that favored state-based religions which appeared in the cases. In short, if the case involved a religion which was well-represented in the judges' home states, then the activist judges were more likely than the non-activists to render a decision that favored that particular religion.

In spite of the fact that they generally tended to be cautious in these decisions, a significant difference does occur in the context of the "judicial constituency" variable. (Yarnold 1988, 1990a) Activist judges were more inclined than non-activists judges to rule in favor of religious groups that appeared in the religious freedoms where those religious denominations were major players in the judges' states in terms of the proportion they represented of the total population of the states. In short, the higher this number, the more likely for activist judges to rule in favor of these groups.

Hence, a general pattern which emerges is that activist judges in the religious liberties cases evaluated here gave ample evidence of their political survival skills. They skillfully maneuvered in these cases so that they were not seemingly captured by any political force, including their parties, and pro and anti-religion groups.

The only exception once again, was for the judicial constituency measures, with activist judges taking into account the religious composition of their states before entering a decision.

This last exception is an important one, since it indicates that in a court which otherwise is removed and detached from political factors, we nevertheless have a certain category of judges, namely the political activists, affording some representation to these major religious interests and groups within their home states. It indicates also that regardless of the distance that is placed between the federal courts and their larger political culture, the greatest survivors in U.S. politics--the political activists--who were later appointed to the federal bench, still felt some pressures from the political environment. Perhaps there is a commonplace insight among political activists turned circuit courts of appeals judges that one cannot, ultimately rule too unpopularly, particularly in an area (religious liberties) that is characterized most often by "intense" preferences among the U.S. public.

Although the circuit courts of appeals, in religious freedoms cases, were generally detached even among the political activists from their external and internal political environment, only the activist judges engaged in representative decision making with respect to their links to their judicial constituents in the religious freedoms cases.

Chapter 7

DID CIRCUIT COURTS OF APPEALS JUDGES OVERCOME THEIR OWN RELIGIONS IN CASES INVOLVING RELIGIOUS LIBERTIES? 1970-1990

This project evaluates, for the period of 1970-1990, decision making by the federal circuit courts in cases which concern religious liberties, protected by the First Amendment of the U.S. Constitution. Specifically, for 1970-1980, the analysis concentrates on federal court cases which deal with the free exercise and establishment clauses of the First Amendment. The research is at the circuit courts of appeals level.

The research examines whether the outcome in these cases (defined as a pro-religion decision) is related to the judges' religious affiliations (or lack of religious faith), and whether litigants were helped by the fact that they shared the same religions as the judges who adjudicated the cases. The religious affiliations which are included in the analysis are as follows: Methodist, Presbyterian, Baptist, Christian, Protestant, Episcopalian, Catholic, Lutheran, Jewish, Disciples of Christ, Church of Christ, and non-religious.

Religious Freedoms and the Federal Courts

Unlike the other "fundamental" rights contained in the First Amendment to the U.S. Constitution, including freedom of speech, press and assembly, which are arguably necessary to the functioning of a representative democracy, the free exercise and establishment clauses of the same amendment are fundamental not due to political necessity but due to historical accident: the fact that so many of the colonists had fled religious persecution in other countries. This is not meant to imply that the religious freedoms clauses of the First Amendment are secondary in any way to the others, it is instead to suggest the vital importance of religious liberty in our constitutional schema, grounded as it is in our nation's history, customs, and political culture.

Although immigrants to the United States may have often been united in their search for religious freedom, it has also been the case that religious differences in this country have led to division. Religious groups were often segregated economically, politically, socially, and even geographically (Kosmin and Lachman 1993). Underlying the debate were fundamental questions which were to guide men and women to truth, morality, justice, and knowledge of their creator. Each religious group unfortunately, tended to answer these fundamental questions with highly or slightly idiosyncratic principles. As a result, debates within the religious community were often filled with friction. To make matters worse, also entering the debate were those who insisted that they had no religious belief and did not want the state to proselytize them in any manner.

The federal courts were given the task of making order out of this disorder, through their apolitical, objective, and almost scientific interpretation of the free exercise and establishment clauses of the First Amendment. Needless to say, their interpretations of the religious freedoms clauses in specific cases has engendered even more debate, within the legal community, among legal scholars,

among the press, policy makers, and the general public. Not surprisingly, there are many critics. And the criticism seems to be warranted at times, when after reviewing cases in perhaps a course on constitutional law, one finds that the rules which emanate from the federal courts in cases dealing with religious freedoms seem to change, are often unclear, conflicting, and impossible to reconcile. A frantic law student studying for a test may surmise unhappily, "perhaps there are no rules."

Although the legal community has been quite thorough in its doctrinal analysis of court cases involving religious liberties (Tribe 1988, Gey 1990, Laycock 1991, Brown 1993, Choper 1995), the same cannot be said of the public law area. To date, relatively few public law analyses of cases involving the free exercise and establishment clauses of the First Amendment have been conducted. Another general observation is that much of the research in the public law area has focused upon the U.S. Supreme Court, and not on the lower federal courts (Shapiro 1993). There have been few, if any, similar analyses of the extent to which federal appeals court judges have overcome their own religious positions or backgrounds in their rulings in religious liberties cases.

For these reasons, the proposed research is not likely to be redundant.

The research utilizes for its purposes federal circuit courts of appeals cases which deal with the free exercise and establishment clauses.

DATA AND METHODS

Official Reporters (Federal Reporters) were used to gather cases for this analysis. The cases included for two decades, from 1970-1990. The total data set is 1,356 appeals court judges decisions rendered during the period. The dependent variable is: is the decision beneficial to religion (a dichotomous dependent variable)? Information on judges' religious affiliations, or the fact that they are non-religious, is gathered from *Judicial Staff Directory* (Brownson 1991), and from another source book, *The American Bench* (Lichterman 1978).

Since the dependent variable is dichotomous (whether the outcome is pro-religion) and there are multiple independent variables, statistical analysis will involve the use of probit. Probit analysis has been employed in similar research contexts. (Segal 1984; Wenner and Dutter 1988, Yarnold 1990a, 1991a.)

FINDINGS

Table I shows the results of probit analysis. The data set included 1,356 cases.

Two of the variables are statistically significant: both Catholic and Baptist appeals court judges were more likely to rule in a pro-religion fashion. Although not significant, Lutheran judges were the only judges likely to take an anti-religion position, while assuming a pro-religion position, though also not significant, were the following judges: Methodists, Presbyterians, Christians, Protestants, Episcopalians, Jewish, Disciples of Christ, and Church of Christ. Being not religious did not make a significant difference in the outcome, since the non-religious still, in general, adopted a pro-religion position. The fact that judges were of the same denomination as the ones concerned in the cases did not significantly increase the chances of winning, though it did make a pro-religion decision more likely.

DISCUSSION

Baptist and Catholic judges were more likely to render a decision that was pro-religion in cases involving religious liberties than were other judges. Most of the other denominations surveyed also supported a pro-religion position, but their support was not at a statistically significant level. Not all religious denominations followed the pro-religion lead, however. Judges who were Lutherans were more likely to enter decisions that were anti-religion, though this again was not significant.

Hence, most of the judges did, in fact overcome their own religious predilections in these cases, with the only exception of Baptist and Catholic judges. But even when the variables did not reach statistical significance, patterns emerge which suggest that judges affiliated with religions which have endured minority status (Jewish, Baptists, Catholics) tend to be more supportive of religious liberties claims in the federal courts than judges affiliated with mainline Protestant denominations.

In a country which has traditionally been the home to those fleeing religious persecution, it is arguably appropriate that the judges of the U.S. circuit courts of appeals reflected a plurality of religions and religious philosophies which were, ultimately, reflected in the decisions in these cases.

To those who tend to be more concerned with free exercise by this country's many religions, this outcome may be perfectly appropriate. To the extent that pluralism may be achieved in the world of judicial politics, it is appropriate that different religious philosophies had their say on questions of the greatest concern to them: religious liberties. Further, since the myth of federal court objectivity on the basis of their lifetime appointments, has been largely discarded by those in the public law community and by legal realists, and it is widely conceded among judicial analysts that the federal courts are simply policy makers, then the question becomes:

what are the appropriate policies for the federal courts to follow in these cases? It may be thus appropriate that certain judges adopt a zealous position in favor of religious freedoms, while others, as we observe, have varying amounts of support. Further, to the extent that the federal appeals courts are greatly distanced from the judicial constituencies they serve, some measure of representation is afforded to the various religious communities and groups within their areas if some circuit court judges, Catholics and Baptists, adopt a pro-religion position.

To those who are more concerned with the non-establishment mandate of the First Amendment, these results may be troubling. The objective federal bench was seemingly pulled by the various religious philosophies of its constituent judges, and thus absconded its responsibility of ensuring that a "wall of separation" exists between state and religion. Indeed, the wall is exposed as nothing but a veneer or convenient judicial metaphor which masks, as always, a highly amorphous institution with enormous power and discretion.

Table 1
Probit Estimates for Circuit Courts Of Appeals Judges' Religious Affiliations In Religious Liberties Cases, 1970-1990
Dependent Variable: Decision Was Pro-Religion

Variable	Maximum Likelihood Error (MLE)	Standard Estimate (S.E.)	MLE/S.E
Constant	4.48	.17	26.30
Is Judge Non-Religious?	.12	.18	.67
Same Religion?	.27	.21	1.32
Methodist	.29	.23	1.28
Presbyterian	.16	.20	.79
Baptist	.51	.28	1.77*
Christian	.27	.44	.62
Protestant	.25	.22	1.11
Episcopalian	.25	.19	1.33
Catholic	.33	.19	1.76*
Lutheran	-.62	.59	-1.06
Jewish	.31	.21	1.48
Disciples of Christ	4.22	25.28	.17
Church of Christ	.09	.77	.12

Chi-Square = 1354.9 DF = 1342 P = .39
N = 1,356
* Significant at .05.

Chapter 8

FACTORS RELATED TO OUTCOMES IN RELIGIOUS FREEDOMS CASES, FEDERAL APPEALS COURTS: 1970-1990

This project evaluates, for the period of 1970-1990, decision making by the federal circuit courts of appeals in cases which concern religious liberties, protected by the First Amendment of the U.S. Constitution. Specifically, for these two decades, the analysis concentrates on federal court cases which deal with the free exercise and establishment clauses of the First Amendment. The research is at the circuit court of appeals level. Yarnold (1990, 1992, 1995c, N.d.) has argued in previous research that political variables (including the partisanship of judges, the presumed desires of "judicial constituents" and the involvement of interest groups in litigation) may be significantly related to judicial decision making when the issue is a "major" issue and/or when powerful groups are interested in the outcome of the case. Since cases involving religious freedoms are major, controversial, and well-publicized cases, this analysis will serve as a good test of the organizing framework for politicized judicial decision making. Similarly, it was hypothesized that region might be significantly related to judicial outcomes when the issue considered by the courts is one with high ideological content (Yarnold 1992, 1995a, 1995c, N.d.). Once again, the religious freedoms cases will serve as a good test of this proposition.

In addition to examining the partisanship of judges, interest group involvement, and judicial constituents, it also divides judges into either activist judges (on the basis of their prior political and administrative positions) or non-activist and attempts to assess whether political activism is related to a more supportive posture toward religious freedom. In addition to improving the political analysis of court cases, the research includes as control variables whether the outcome in these cases is related to the judges' religious affiliations (or lack of religious faith), the ages of the judges, and their gender.

Religious Freedoms and the Federal Courts

Unlike the other "fundamental" rights contained in the First Amendment to the U.S. Constitution, including freedom of speech, press and assembly, which are arguably necessary to the functioning of a representative democracy on the basis that they serve to provide for a more enlightened and informed electorate, the free exercise and establishment clauses of the same amendment are fundamental not due to political necessity but due to historical accident: the fact that so many of the colonists had fled religious persecution in other countries. This is not meant to imply that the religious freedoms clauses of the First Amendment are secondary in any way to the others, it is instead to suggest the vital importance of religious liberty in our constitutional schema, grounded as it is in our nation's history, customs, and political culture.

Although immigrants to the United States may have often been united in their search for religious freedom, it has also been the case that religious differences in this country have led to division.

Religious groups were often segregated economically, politically, socially, and even geographically (Kosmin and Lachman 1993). Underlying the debate were fundamental questions which were to guide men and women to truth, morality, justice, and knowledge of their creator. Each religious group unfortunately, tended to answer these fundamental questions with highly or slightly idiosyncratic principles. As a result, debates within the religious community were often filled with friction. To make matters worse, also entering the debate were those who insisted that they had no religious belief and did not want the state to proselytize them in any manner.

The federal courts were given the task of making order out of this disorder, through their presumably apolitical and objective interpretation of the free exercise and establishment clauses of the First Amendment. Needless to say, their interpretations of the religious freedoms clauses in specific cases has engendered even more debate, within the legal community, among legal scholars, among the press, policy makers, and the general public. Not surprisingly, there are many critics. And the criticism seems to be warranted at times, when after reviewing cases in perhaps a course on constitutional law, one finds that the rules which emanate from the federal courts in cases dealing with religious freedoms seem to change, are often unclear, conflicting, and impossible to reconcile. A frantic law student studying for a test may surmise unhappily, "perhaps there are no rules."

Although the legal community has been quite thorough in its doctrinal analysis of court cases involving religious liberties (Tribe 1988, Gey 1990, Laycock 1991, Brown 1993, Choper 1995), the same cannot be said of the public law area. To date, relatively few public law analyses of cases involving the free exercise and establishment clauses of the First Amendment have been conducted. Another general observation is that much of the research in the public law area has focused upon the U.S. Supreme Court, and not on the lower federal courts (Shapiro 1993). For these reasons, the proposed research is not likely to be redundant.

The research will utilize for its purposes federal circuit court of appeals cases which deal with the free exercise and establishment clauses. There are several reasons for dealing with both clauses simultaneously. The first is pragmatic: most judicial decisions which deal with religious liberties discuss both clauses. Second, from a more theoretical perspective, the free exercise and establishment clauses share a common purpose, namely protecting the liberties of religious individuals and the non-religious. Finally, it is based upon an underlying skepticism about the importance of rules, and even the existence of rules, concepts which have emerged in the public law area.

HYPOTHESES

The project draws upon Yarnold's prior work in the public law area, which has been concerned with the question of why federal court outcomes are related to political factors (including interest group involvement in litigation, the partisanship of judges, and the preferences of judicial constituencies), and to the environment, while in other types of cases political factors do not reach the level of statistical significance (Yarnold 1990a, 1990b, 1991, 1992, 1994a, 1994b, 1995a, 1995b, 1995c, N.d.). Drawing upon this research and that of others, an organizing framework was developed (Yarnold 1992, 1995c, N.d.) which predicts that federal courts, in spite of lifetime appointments, are likely to respond to political factors when the case in question involves a "major issue," defined as an issue that is regularly reported by the media, receives public scrutiny, and tends to conform with divisions between the Democratic and Republican parties. This, incidentally, is an adaptation of Page et. al's (1983) earlier work on congressional decision making. Hence, in Yarnold's previous research, in asylum and refugee appeals from 1980-1987 and abortion cases adjudicated during the period 1973-1990, both dealing with major issues, the outcomes were related to political factors.

In contrast, in cases dealing with international extradition, judicial outcomes were not related to the same political factors (interest group involvement, judicial constituents, and partisanship). Although these types of cases are of immense interest to certain ethnic groups in the United States, they are not well-publicized and not likely to divide the electorate along partisan lines. Hence, international extradition is not, arguably, a major issue. However, it was observed that the individuals who were subject to extradition requests were much more likely to prevail if they were linked to the IRA, while those linked to the PLO were much less likely to prevail. It was argued that the Irish lobby in the U.S. is much stronger than the Palestinian lobby. Hence, a second part of the model predicts that other cases in which judicial outcomes may be related to political factors are those which involve non-major issues, but are nevertheless of interest to major groups in the U.S.

In most of Yarnold's research, region was also included in the analysis. However, in asylum and international extradition cases, region was not significant. In contrast, in many analyses region has been found to be significantly related to judicial outcomes, for example, in environmental litigation (Wenner 1982; Wenner and Dutter 1988) and race relations cases (Richardson and Vines 1978). To reconcile these disparate findings, Yarnold (1992, 1995c) suggested that region might be most likely to be significant in cases which deal with a highly ideological issue, such as abortion. Hence, in fact, in abortion cases, region was found to be significantly related to the outcome (Yarnold 1995a, 1995b).

One of the major research objectives of this study is to test, in the context of religious liberty cases (or cases which involve the free exercise or establishment clauses), clearly cases which involve major issues, the various predictions of the organizing framework for politized judicial decisions. Specifically, are outcomes in these cases related to "political factors" (the involvement of interest groups in litigation, judicial constituents, and the partisanship of judges)? Further, since these cases are also highly ideological, are the outcomes significantly related to region? Of course, if the predictions are unsupported by the analysis, the hope is then to fashion a new or modified one in light of the findings.

It is also anticipated that the power of the model will be enhanced by the addition of the "political activism" inquiry. In other words, it is anticipated that judges who were political activists prior to their ascent to the federal bench (they held political and/or appointive office), will decide the religious freedoms cases differently from those who were not political activists.

In addition to improving the political analysis of court cases, the research also examines other facets of the judicial environment which may also help to understand decisions in cases involving religious liberties. The dependent variable cases is whether the judicial decision is one which is pro-religion. The additional control variables which are included relate to arguably relevant factors relating to the judges including: their religious affiliations (or lack of religious belief), their ages, and their gender.

DATA AND METHODS

Official Reporters (the Federal Reporters) were used to gather cases for this analysis. The cases included here are for two decades, from 1970-1990. The total data set is 466 circuit courts of appeals cases decided during this period. The dependent variable in the public law analysis of court cases is: is the decision beneficial to religion (a dichotomous dependent variable)? Specifically, cases usually involve one or more religious denominations and if the decision benefits the specific denomination, then the decision is coded as "pro-religion."

There is no attempt to evaluate whether the decision benefited religion in a more holistic or general sense since this would lead to great difficulty in coding the dependent variable, and lend itself to inappropriate subjective "guesses" about the extent to which religion in general is benefited by a particular judicial outcome. The more conservative approach adopted here--namely limiting the analysis to whether religious individuals and organizations who were litigants in these cases prevailed--has advantages in terms of conceptual clarity and limiting the scope of the inquiry. This conservative approach, however, also has disadvantages, since a number of cases were excluded from the analysis as they made no specific mention of a particular religious organization.

Information on interest group involvement in the cases is derived from reading the cases, which typically list the interest groups. Information on the partisan affiliations of judges, their religions (or lack of religious affiliation), their ages, and their gender is gathered from a Judicial Staff Directory (Brownson 1991), and from another source book, The American Bench (Lichterman 1978). These sources were also used to determine whether the judges are political activists, with judges gaining this designation if, in their pre-appointment activities, they held one or more elective or appointive office. Wenner's (1982; 1988) typology of region is used for coding the region variable in this analysis. The "judicial constituency" variable in these cases was measured as follows: the case was scanned to determine which religion was in issue. For example, a case involving a use of public funds for a Papal Mass was coded:

Roman Catholic. Most of the cases are much more straightforward, however, involving an individual who is either filing an action or defending an action and indicates his or her religious affiliation. In other instances, as where an ordinance allows for the maintenance of a lighted cross in a public park, there is usually no specific religion involved but it will fall into the category of "general

Christian." In these cases, there has been no attempt to categorize the religion. After ascertaining the religion in dispute, such as Roman Catholic, the state in which the case was adjudicated is identified. From this, the judicial constituency variable is measured as: percentage of the state population which is the religion in question. Hence if the home state of the case were Rhode Island, and the case involved Roman Catholics, a measure was made of the percentage of the population in Rhode Island in 1990 that was Catholic: 61.7% The information on the religious populations within states was derived from Religion in Contemporary American Society, by Kosmin and Lachman (Crown Publishers, Inc. 1993). Once again, as in the case of the dependent variable, if there is no specific mention in the case of a religious denomination, the case was excluded from the analysis.

Since circuit courts of appeals consist of panels of three judges, where appropriate, the independent variables were measured in an aggregate manner. For example, for the variable relating to the religious affiliations of the judges, the measure is, "what percentage of the judges belong to a religious denomination (as indicated in judicial biographies)?" For the measure of gender, "what percentage of the judges are male?" Similarly, with regard to the ages of the judges, we simply have the average ages of the three judges involved in the case. With the "Republican" measure, we measure the "percentage of judges who are members of the Republican Party." For the "Activism" measure, we list the "percentage of judges who were political activists in their pre-appointment activities." The last variable in which this becomes an issue is for the judicial constituency measure of the extent to which the religion involved in case is high relative to total state population. The religion is measured for all three states in which judges reside, and an average measure is compiled for this variable.

Since the dependent variable is dichotomous (whether the outcome is pro-religion) and there are multiple independent variables, statistical analysis involves the use of probit. Probit analysis has been employed is similar research contexts. (Segal 1984; Wenner and Dutter 1988, Yarnold 1990a, 1991a.)

The independent variables are as follows: the average ages of the judges at the time a decision is rendered; percentage of judges that are male; percentage of judges that are religious; percentage of judges that are political activists; percentage of judges that belong to the Republican Party; are there pro-religion interest groups involved in the case; are there anti-religion interest groups in the case; what is the percentage, for all three states of judges, in 1990 of the judges' states that is of the same religion that appears in the case; is the case presided over by federal courts in the South; the Midwest; the Northeast; or the West?

Table 1
Probit Estimates for Federal Circuit Court of Appeals Religious Liberties Cases, 1970-1990
Dependent Variable: Decision Was Pro-Religion

Variable	Maximum Likelihood Error (MLE)	Standard Estimate (S.E.)	MLE/S.E.
Constant	5.99	.94	6.36
Are Judge Religious?	.01	.01	.99
Age of Judges	- .01	.01	- 1.08
Are Judges Male?	- .01	.01	- .92
Are Judges Republican?	- .01	.01	- .90
Are Judges Activists ?	.01	.01	.09
Are There Pro-Religion Groups?	- .31	.16	- 1.90*

Are There Anti-Religion Groups?	- .14	.20	- .67
% Judges' State Populations 1990 Same Religion As in Case	.01	.01	1.30
South	.16	.23	.69
Midwest	- .30	.22	- 1.40
Northeast	.14	.23	.59

Chi-Square = 285.8 DF = 273 P = .33
N = 285
* Significant at .05.

FINDINGS

Table I shows the results of probit analysis. One deficiency with probit is that it deletes cases that have missing data, and in this analysis, missing data occurred primarily in connection with three variables: the dependent variable, namely whether the decision benefited the particular religion(s) involved in the case, and two independent variables: the religion involved in the case (for the purpose of the "judicial constituency" measure) and the religious affiliations of the judges. The first two problems arose simply because the opinions filed by judges did not mention a religion. The third deficiency arose because judges are reluctant to provide their religious affiliations to judicial biographers. These problems, are however, unavoidable. Hence, though the initial data set included 466 cases, 181 cases were rejected due to missing data, and 285 cases remain. There is no reason to suspect any systematic bias in the data as a result of the deletion of cases, since they were not deliberate and occurred due to chance. Hence, the remaining cases are likely representative of the total population of cases.

Only one variable is statistically significant: the involvement of pro-religion interest groups in the litigation, and there is an inverse relationship between pro-religion outcomes and pro-religion groups. At a statistically significant level, pro-religion groups are likely to lose. Specifically, probit analysis generates parameter estimates through the maximum likelihood estimation (MLE) method, which assumes that the error term is normally distributed. The analysis has generated MLE estimates for each independent variable which represent the amount of change produced in the cumulative normal probability function by a one unit change in an independent variable. The MLE's divided by their standard errors approximate a normal distribution so it is possible to test whether the independent variables are significant, when controlling for other independent variables.

Hence, the MLE/SE statistic allows us to know the probability of seeing the observed results. To say that something is significant is to make the statement that, when controlling for all of the other variables, these variables still count (the significant ones). Further, it is likely that the results are not due to chance alone. An MLE/SE estimate which is significant at the .05 level means that there is only five percent or lower chance of generating these results due to chance alone.

DISCUSSION

The main prediction of the organizing framework for politicized judicial decision making is that in federal court cases that involve major, publicized issues, political factors will be related to the outcome. What one observes is that in cases dealing with religious liberties, the involvement of pro-religion groups in litigation--a political factor--is significantly related to the outcome in these cases. More specifically, the involvement of pro-religion groups in litigation was significantly and inversely related to a pro-religion decision by the federal circuit courts of appeals in cases dealing with the free exercise and establishment clauses of the First Amendment. Hence, the most important hypothesis of the organizing framework is supported (or not rejected) in the analysis.

On a more substantive level, however, when one makes a comparison of the appeals decisions in these cases with the earlier decisions of the district courts, (Yarnold 1995c, N.d.), major differences emerge. And, the most important difference is that the district courts tended to give pro-religion wins to the pro-religion groups while exactly the opposite is true for the circuit courts of appeals during the two-decade period, 1970-1990. The appeals courts, at a statistically significant level, ruled against the pro-religion groups. To the extent that the district courts handed gains to the pro-religion groups which appeared before them, the circuit court of appeals reversed this policy direction, handing out losses to pro-religion groups at even higher levels than the district court granted wins.

Given the fact that this was the only significant variable in the appeals cases involving religious liberties cases, to the extent that one may extrapolate some policy direction in these various courts, the district courts were favorably disposed toward pro-religion groups while the appeals courts overwhelmingly were opposed to the same groups. The appeals judges were not closely associated with these pro-religion groups by virtue of the fact that they often came from states outside of the pro-religion groups' states of domicile.

Other differences also emerge. The appeals courts were not linked to regional variations. Judges in the North, South, and West tended to rule in a pro-religion way, while courts in the Midwest tended to rule in an anti-religion manner, but none of these are significant. District courts located in the Midwest and the South were, at a significant level, associated with anti-religion outcomes. The circuit courts of appeals were arguably not as clearly linked to their local environments as were the district courts.

In the district court cases, there were also gender differences with male judges significantly more likely to enter a pro-religion decision than female judges. However, by the time we reach the level of the circuit courts of appeals, the differences are eliminated as male judges actually are more likely to enter an anti-religion decision than the female appeals judges, though this is not significant.

There were two different sets of wars going on in these religious freedoms cases adjudicated by the federal district courts and circuit courts of appeals during the two decade period between 1970-1990. One war was carried on between the pro-and anti-religious groups and individuals which were involved as litigants during this period. The second type of war was between the different levels of the courts, namely district and appeals.

In terms of the war between the litigants, the federal district courts overwhelmingly favored pro-religion groups over anti-religion groups.

The second type of war which emerged in the religious freedoms cases adjudicated 1970-1990 was between two levels of the federal judiciary: the district courts and the circuit courts of appeals. While the district courts were characterized as populist, representative institutions, with close linkages to their regions, and with male political activist judges overwhelmingly granting victories to pro-religion groups, the circuit courts of appeals completely reversed the policy making direction of the lower federal courts. The appeals courts lost their representative nature as their links to their environments eroded and the major policy effect of the federal circuit courts of appeals was to undo the pro-religion group outcomes of the district courts. The same pro-religion groups which found victories at the level of the district court found losses at the hands of the circuit courts of appeals.

Chapter 9

VIEWING THE "INNER CIRCLE": U.S. SUPREME COURT JUSTICES IN RELIGIOUS FREEDOMS CASES, 1970-1990

This part moves on to an evaluation of decisions of the U.S. Supreme Court in cases which concern religious liberties, namely either the free exercise or non-establishment clause of the 1st Amendment to the U.S. Constitution. The time span involved is two decades, from 1970-1990.

Perhaps the greatest insight into the politicized nature of the federal courts have been offered by Baum (1989). In his work on the lower federal courts and the U.S. Supreme Court, he points out that these courts are immersed in politics in spite of the fact that they are presumably shielded from these influences due to their lifetime appointments.

However, Baum (1989) notes that these judges have, for the most part, been selected based upon their prior work for political parties, and that almost all of the judges are of the same political party as their appointing Presidents. He went on to analyze characteristics of typical federal judges and found that most of these judges have held political and/or appointive office prior to their selection to the federal judiciary.

In this twenty-year survey of U.S. Supreme Court justices involved in religious freedoms cases, the same observations hold. Namely, the justices had often, for example served as state court judges, served either in state legislatures or in Congress, or served as the Attorney Generals for their states. Further, this politicized activity was the rule rather than the exception. This study classified justices as "political activists" if they had held one or more political or appointive office prior to their appointment. Sixty-eight (68%) of the justices were found to be political activists. Those who were not activists were often private attorneys with distinguished records, many of whom had held positions on bar organizations external to mainstream U.S. politics. Hence, they were legal activists rather than political activists. There was the occasional law professor who was also appointed who was not a political activist.

Another interesting note is that in 50% of the cases involved in the survey, the justices were involved in partisan decision-making. So, for example, Republican justices would decide cases in favor of religious liberties and Democratic justices would decide against religious liberties.

Given the fact that most of the justices have had long careers in partisan politics prior to their appointment to the federal bench, it is not surprising that they are not a particularly young group. For the Supreme Court justices, their ages ranged from 48 to 87, and the mode age was 65.

In spite of the fact that in recent years, women roughly equal men in numbers in terms of admissions to law schools, in the religious freedoms cases surveyed here, 94% of the justices were men, while only 5% were women. The Court also seems to have been largely a Republican institution during 1970-1990, with 74%% of the justices belonging to the Republican Party, while only 26% of the justices were members of the Democratic Party.

Given the salience of these issues to major organized religious groups, it is not surprising there was heavy involvement in these cases of pro-religion interest groups, or groups who supported the 1st Amendment rights of a particular religion. 80% percent of these cases involved pro-religion groups. The pro-religion groups included not only religious organizations, but other actors, such as civil liberties groups. Since some of these cases involved indigent prisoners who claimed their religious rights had been violated by prison officials, legal aid groups often also made their appearance, as well as ad-hoc citizens groups which argued that, for example, the public schools were violating the religious freedoms of their students. In spite of this high involvement of pro-religion groups in the litigation, the decisions rendered by the U.S. Supreme Court during this period granted pro-religion decisions in only 47% of the cases.

More successful during this period were the anti-religion forces, who had anti-religion decisions rendered in 53% of the cases, in spite of the lower involvement of the anti-religion forces at the level of the Supreme Court. Fifty-four percent of the religious freedoms cases also involved anti-religion groups, and these included, for example, civil liberties groups, organizations committed to preventing the intermixture of religion with public institutions, labor unions which argued that workers should be forced to pay union dues and/or join unions in spite of the fact that their religions proscribed such activities, and teacher's unions that battled to ensure that funds allocated to public schools should be restricted to public schools and not expended on religious schools.

Somewhat anomalous is that, in spite of their anti-religion decisions, one-hundred percent (100%) of the justices were religious, or indicated that they belonged to a religious denomination.

The religion cases involved mostly Midwestern justices (44% of the cases) and justices from the South (27% of the cases). Northern justices were involved in 16% of the cases, while only 12% of the cases involved justices from the West.

In terms of their rank, The Supreme Court justices were overwhelmingly Episcopalians, appearing in 32%% of the cases, followed, in descending order, by Presbyterians (20.5%), Catholics (16%), Methodists (11% 8%), Lutherans (10%), Protestants (9%), and Baptist (.8%) justices.

Chapter 10

DID ACTIVIST SUPREME COURT JUSTICES DECIDE CASES INVOLVING RELIGIOUS LIBERTIES DIFFERENTLY THAN NON-ACTIVIST JUSTICES? 1970-1990

ABSTRACT

This project evaluates, for the period of 1970-1990, decision making by the U.S. Supreme Court in cases dealing with religious liberties, or cases in which the establishment and/or free exercise clause of the 1st Amendment are at issue. The specific research question is whether there was significant variance in the decision making of activist versus non-activist judges.

The statistical analysis reveals that there are no significant differences in the way activist judges and non-activist judges in the U.S. Supreme Court decide the religious freedoms cases. Specifically, activist judges were more likely to rule in favor of judicial constituents, earlier defined as groups or political forces which are significant players in the judges' states (Yarnold 1888, 1990a, 1990b). The judicial constituency in the religious freedoms cases were identified as the religious denominations which appeared in the cases, and a measure was taken of the relative size of these religious denominations in the nine "home states" (states in which the justices were born) representing the nine different justices involved in the panels. Political activists appeals court judges were more likely to rule in favor of the denominations involved in a case where the denominations represented a relatively sizable portion of the populations in the three states.

But this was not significant.

Activist Supreme Court justices also were tended to vote against their partisan ties, and cautiously awarded losses to both the pro-religion and the anti-religion groups involved in the cases.

This project evaluates, for the period of 1970-1990, decision making by the U.S. Supreme Court in cases which concern religious liberties, protected by the First Amendment of the U.S. Constitution. Specifically, the analysis concentrates on federal court cases which deal with the free exercise and establishment clauses of the First Amendment.

The research is at the U.S. Supreme Court level, and examines whether activist judges were more likely than non-activist judges to render decisions in these cases that were responsive to the partisanship of the judges, the participation of both pro- and anti-religion groups, and the judicial constituencies which are represented in these cases.

RELIGIOUS FREEDOMS AND THE FEDERAL COURTS

Unlike the other "fundamental" rights contained in the First Amendment to the U.S. Constitution, including freedom of speech, press and assembly, which are arguably necessary to the functioning of a representative democracy, the free exercise and establishment clauses of the same amendment are fundamental not due to political necessity but due to historical accident: the fact that so many of the colonists had fled religious persecution in other countries. This is not meant to imply that the religious freedoms clauses of the First Amendment are secondary in any way to the others, it is instead to suggest the vital importance of religious liberty in our constitutional schema, grounded as it is in our nation's history, customs, and political culture.

Although immigrants to the United States may have often been united in their search for religious freedom, it has also been the case that religious differences in this country have led to division. Religious groups were often segregated economically, politically, socially, and even geographically (Kosmin and Lachman 1993). Underlying the debate were fundamental questions which were to guide men and women to truth, morality, justice, and knowledge of their creator. Each religious group unfortunately, tended to answer these fundamental questions with highly or slightly idiosyncratic principles. As a result, debates within the religious community were often filled with friction. To make matters worse, also entering the debate were those who insisted that they had no religious belief and did not want the state to proselytize them in any manner.

The federal courts were given the task of making order out of this disorder, through their apolitical, objective, and almost scientific interpretation of the free exercise and establishment clauses of the First Amendment. Needless to say, their interpretations of the religious freedoms clauses in specific cases has engendered even more debate, within the legal community, among legal scholars, among the press, policy makers, and the general public. Not surprisingly, there are many critics. And the criticism seems to be warranted at times, when after reviewing cases in perhaps a course on constitutional law, one finds that the rules which emanate from the federal courts in cases dealing with religious freedoms seem to change, are often unclear, conflicting, and impossible to reconcile. A frantic law student studying for a test may surmise unhappily, "perhaps there are no rules."

Although the legal community has been quite thorough in its doctrinal analysis of court cases involving religious liberties (Tribe 1988, Gey 1990, Laycock 1991, Brown 1993, Choper 1995), the same cannot be said of the public law area. To date, relatively few public law analyses of cases involving the free exercise and establishment clauses of the First Amendment have been conducted. There have been few, if any, similar analyses of whether activist U.S. Supreme Court justices are more or less responsive in their decision making than non-activist judges to their partisan affiliations, the involvement of pro-and anti-religion groups, and the presumed desires of their judicial constituents. For these reasons, the proposed research is not likely to be redundant.

The research utilizes for its purposes U.S. Supreme Court cases which deal with the free exercise and establishment clauses.

DATA AND METHODS

Official Reporters (U.S. Supreme Court Reports) were used to gather cases for this analysis. The cases included here are for two decades, from 1970 to 1990. The total data set is 629 individual votes of Justices (from 76 cases) decided during this period. The dependent variable is: is the judge an activist (a dichotomous dependent variable)? Information on judicial activism is gathered from Judicial Staff Directory (Brownson 1991), and from another source book, The American Bench (Lichterman 1978). Judges were deemed to be activists if they held one or more political and/or appointive offices prior to their appointment to the federal bench. Since the courts here consist of panels of nine judges, a measure was made for each justice on the activism measure. The independent variables relating to partisanship, pro-religion interest group litigation, anti-religion interest group litigation, and the preferences of judicial constituents, were coded in the following manner. The judge was deemed to have responded to his or her party ties if he or she were a Republican judge and decided the case in a pro-religion manner, and if he or she were a Democratic judge and decided the case in an anti-religion manner.

For the pro-interest group measure, judges were deemed to have entered a pro-religious group decision in a case if the pro-religion group won the case (and a pro-religion decision was entered). Anti-religious groups were also recorded as being successful litigants if they won their case (and thus an anti-religion decision was entered). To compute the judicial constituency measure, for each case, a measure was taken of the religious affiliations that were involved in the case, for example, Mormons. We used for this analysis the states within which the justices were born. Since each judge was born within a particular state, a measure was taken of the percentage of that state's population which shares the same religion as the one involved in the case. For example, if the case involved Catholics and the justice was born in New York, the percentage of Catholics in New York in 1990 was (hypothetically) 44.3%.

In this way one hopes to estimate the extent to which activist Supreme Court justices in these cases were responsive to the preferences of various religious affiliations within their states. And, of course, whether there is a marked difference between activist and non-activist judges in this regard. Information on the religious compositions within states was gathered from Kosmin and Lachman (1993).

Since the dependent variable is dichotomous (whether the judge is an activist) and there are multiple independent variables, statistical analysis will involve the use of probit. Probit analysis has been employed similar research contexts. (Segal 1984; Wenner and Dutter 1988, Yarnold 1990a, 1991a.)

Findings

Table I shows the results of probit analysis. The initial data set included 629 votes, 137 of the votes were rejected due to missing data, and 492 votes remain.

None of the variables is statistically significant.

Judges who were activists were more likely than the non-activists to render a decision that was anti-partisan, hence, for example, a Republican judge would enter an anti-religion decision, but this was not significant. Activist judges were also more likely than the non-activists to award losses to pro-religion groups, but again, this is not significant. Though also not significant, activist judges were also somewhat more likely than the non-activists to award "losses" to the anti-religion groups.

The only variable which is close to being statistically significant is the judicial constituency measure in these cases. Judges who were activists were more likely than the non-activists to respond positively to the fact that the religions which appeared in the cases were well-represented in terms of total state populations, within the judges' states.

Discussion

Given their lifetime of immersion in partisan politics, it is not at all surprising that activist judges, or judges who had held either elective or appointive office prior to their appointment to the federal bench, did not display any major patterns that would distinguish them in any significant way from the non-activist judges. They have crafted well their survival skills in the volatile world of politics and carry these skills with mastery to their new positions in the federal courts. Hence, not surprisingly, the activists tended to distance themselves from their parties, but would not completely sever the relationship. Hence, the activists were inclined to rule against their party's position in the religious freedoms cases, but in a most anemic manner. After all, if they contemplate further advances within or outside of the federal judiciary, it is useful to have the home party to call upon when it can render further service.

Similarly, the activist judges, aware of the need to maintain positive relationships with interest groups, did a balancing act between the pro- and the anti-religion groups which became involved in the religious liberties litigation. The activists were slightly more likely to award losses to the pro-religion groups than the non-activists, but this support was so slight as to be almost nonexistent, ensuring no backlash from politically powerful groups within the anti-religion lobby. The activists were also slightly more likely than the non-activists to render losses to the anti-religion groups, including civil liberties groups, but the losses were seemingly lackluster and again, very weak. The groups which appeared in these cases, including, for example, religious organizations and civil liberties groups, are potent actors in judicial appointments, and hence the activist judges carefully split their decisions between the various pro- and anti-religion groups.

Finally, with respect to the judicial constituency measure, the activists were somewhat more likely than the non-activists to render decisions that favored state-based religions which appeared in the cases. In short, if the case involved a religion which was well-represented in the judges' home states, then the activist judges were more likely than the non-activists to render a decision that favored that particular religion. However, this variable was not significant.

Hence, a general pattern which emerges is that activist judges in the religious liberties cases evaluated here gave ample evidence of their political survival skills. They skillfully maneuvered in these cases so that they were not seemingly captured by any political force, including their parties, the pro and anti-religion groups, and their judicial constituents.

Table 1
Probit Estimates for Activist U.S. Supreme Courts Judges In Religious Liberties Cases, 1970-1990
Dependent Variable: Is Judge An Activist?

Variable	Maximum Likelihood Error (MLE)	Standard Estimate (S.E.)	MLE/S.E.
Constant	5.54	.13	42.65
Partisan Decision	-.12	.12	-.97
Pro-Religion Groups	-.07	.16	-.46
Anti-Religion Groups	-.13	.16	-.78
Religious Constituency	.01	.01	1.13

Chi-Square = 491.62 DF = 487 P = .43
N = 492

Chapter 11

DID U.S. SUPREME COURT JUSTICES OVERCOME THEIR OWN RELIGIONS IN CASES INVOLVING RELIGIOUS LIBERTIES? 1970-1990

ABSTRACT

This project represents results from a two decade study (1970-1990) which evaluates U.S Supreme Court decisions in cases involving "religious liberties," or cases dealing with the free exercise and establishment clauses of the First Amendment to the U.S. Constitution. It evaluates whether judges, in their decisions in these cases, overcame their own religious predilections.

The analysis demonstrates that the U.S. Supreme Court justices did not overcome their own religions. In fact, judges who were aligned with the Protestant Church and with the Methodist Church, two Protestant denominations, were significantly more likely than the other judges, as a result of their religious orientations, to favor an anti-religion stance. Episcopalians were also likely to enter an anti-religion decision, but not at a significant level, as were Presbyterian judges. Catholic judges were also negative, but at an extremely low level. Only Baptist judges entered pro-religion votes in these cases, but at a very low level.

U.S. Supreme Court judges also seemed to attempt to reflect an objective posture, ruling in these cases, at a significant level, against their own religious denominations.

This project evaluates, for the period of 1970-1990, decision making by the U.S. Supreme Court in cases which concern religious liberties, protected by the First Amendment of the U.S. Constitution. Specifically, for 1970-1980, the analysis concentrates on cases which deal with the free exercise and establishment clauses of the First Amendment.

The research examines whether the outcome in these cases (defined as a pro-religion decision) is related to the judges' religious affiliations (or lack of religious faith), and whether litigants were helped by the fact that they shared the same religions as the judges who adjudicated the cases. The religious affiliations which are included in the analysis are as follows: Methodist, Presbyterian, Baptist, Protestant, Episcopalian, and Catholic.

RELIGIOUS FREEDOMS AND THE FEDERAL COURTS

Unlike the other "fundamental" rights contained in the First Amendment to the U.S. Constitution, including freedom of speech, press and assembly, which are arguably necessary to the functioning of a representative democracy, the free exercise and establishment clauses of the same amendment are fundamental not due to political necessity but due to historical accident: the fact that so many of the colonists had fled religious persecution in other countries. This is not meant to imply that the religious freedoms clauses of the First Amendment are secondary in any way to the others, it is instead to suggest the vital importance of religious liberty in our constitutional schema, grounded as it is in our nation's history, customs, and political culture.

Although immigrants to the United States may have often been united in their search for religious freedom, it has also been the case that religious differences in this country have led to division. Religious groups were often segregated economically, politically, socially, and even geographically (Kosmin and Lachman 1993). Underlying the debate were fundamental questions which were to guide men and women to truth, morality, justice, and knowledge of their creator. Each religious group unfortunately, tended to answer these fundamental questions with highly or slightly idiosyncratic principles. As a result, debates within the religious community were often filled with friction. To make matters worse, also entering the debate were those who insisted that they had no religious belief and did not want the state to proselytize them in any manner.

The federal courts were given the task of making order out of this disorder, through their apolitical, objective, and almost scientific interpretation of the free exercise and establishment clauses of the First Amendment. Needless to say, their interpretations of the religious freedoms clauses in specific cases has engendered even more debate, within the legal community, among legal scholars, among the press, policy makers, and the general public. Not surprisingly, there are many critics. And the criticism seems to be warranted at times, when after reviewing cases in perhaps a course on constitutional law, one finds that the rules which emanate from the federal courts in cases dealing with religious freedoms seem to change, are often unclear, conflicting, and impossible to reconcile. A frantic law student studying for a test may surmise unhappily, "perhaps there are no rules."

Although the legal community has been quite thorough in its doctrinal analysis of court cases involving religious liberties (Tribe 1988, Gey 1990, Laycock 1991, Brown 1993, Choper 1995), the same cannot be said of the public law area. To date, relatively few public law analyses of cases involving the free exercise and establishment clauses of the First Amendment have been conducted. There have been few, if any, similar analyses of the extent to which U.S. Supreme Court judges have overcome their own religious positions or backgrounds in their rulings in religious liberties cases. For these reasons, the proposed research is not likely to be redundant.

DATA AND METHODS

Official Reporters (U.S Reports) were used to gather cases for this analysis. The cases included for two decades, from 1970-1990. The total data set is drawn from 76 U.S. Supreme Court cases rendered during this period. Specifically, the research focuses upon the individual votes of each of the justices involved in the cases, and the total votes number 624. The dependent variable is: is the decision beneficial to religion (a dichotomous dependent variable)? Information on judges' religious affiliations, or the fact that they are non-religious, is gathered from *Judicial Staff Directory* (Brownson 1991), and from another source book, *The American Bench* (Lichterman 1978).

Since the dependent variable is dichotomous (whether the outcome is pro-religion) and there are multiple independent variables, statistical analysis will involve the use of probit. Probit analysis has been employed is similar research contexts. (Segal 1984; Wenner and Dutter 1988, Yarnold 1990a, 1991a.)

Table 1

Probit Estimates for U.S Supreme Court Judges' Religious Affiliations In Religious Liberties Cases, 1970-1990

Dependent Variable: Decision Was Pro-Religion

Variable	Maximum Likelihood Error (MLE)	Standard Estimate (S.E.)	MLE/S.E.
Constant	5.18	.16	33.12
Same Religion?	- .43	.26	- 1.68*
Methodist	- .36	.22	- 1.66*
Presbyterian	- .16	.19	- .83
Baptist	.07	.59	.12
Protestant	- .69	.24	- 2.95*
Episcopalian	- .19	.18	- 1.04
Catholic	- .12	.21	- .55

Chi-Square = 624.1 DF = 616 P = .40

N = 624

* Significant at .05.

Note: Lutheran judges had to be excluded since there was an insufficient number of cases

FINDINGS

Table I shows the results of probit analysis. The data set included 624 cases.

Three of the variables are statistically significant: both judges affiliated with Protestant Church and Methodist judges were more likely to rule in an anti-religion fashion. Although not significant, Baptist judges were the only judges likely to take a pro-religion position.

The study also wanted to see whether judges decisions were also related to the fact that they were not religious. However, this had to be excluded from the analysis since all of the Supreme Court justices were religious.

A third significant independent variable was that the judges shared the same religious affiliations as the litigants involved in a particular case. Where these denominations were the same, this significantly increased the chances that an anti-religion decision would be entered.

DISCUSSION

Baptist judges were the only judges that were likely to enter a pro-religion decision, though their support was weak and this variable is not statistically significant. The overwhelming tendency of the U.S. Supreme Court in the religious freedoms cases from 1970-1990 was to rule in an anti-religion manner. With the exception of Baptist judges, all of the other denominations supported an anti-religion position. The most severe anti-religion votes were granted by judges who members of the Protestant Church, and this variable is statistically significant. Following next were justices who were members of the Methodist religion, and their anti-religion vote was also statistically significant. Next in line, all insignificant were

Episcopalian judges, Presbyterian judges and Catholic judges. Also operating in the general anti-religion direction of the U.S. Supreme Court was that judges who shared the same religious backgrounds as the litigants involved in these cases overwhelmingly granted these litigants losses, at a statistically significant level.

Hence, in terms of the general inquiry, the judges did not overcome their own religions in these cases, their religious backgrounds tended to make them rule in an anti-religion manner, though this was particularly true for the mainline Protestant denominations: judges who were members of the Protestant Church and Methodists.

But even when the variables did not reach statistical significance, patterns emerge which suggest that judges affiliated with religions which have endured minority status (Baptists, Catholics) tend to be more supportive of religious liberties claims in the federal courts than judges affiliated with mainline Protestant denominations.

In a country which has traditionally been the home to those fleeing religious persecution, one might hope that the judges of the U.S. Supreme Court reflected a plurality of religions and religious philosophies which were, ultimately, reflected in the decisions in these cases.

However, this did not occur;, the decisions of the U.S. Supreme Court reflected only the anti-religion position and constituents, giving absolutely no representation to the pro-religion position and constituents, again, with the sole exception of Baptist judges. The overwhelmingly Protestant judges on the U.S. Supreme Court granted losses to the pro-religion groups and wins only to the anti-religion forces.

Hence, the representation afforded by the U.S. Supreme Court was interestingly, not only incomplete in the sense of missing many of the players, it was absolutely one-sided (in favor of the anti-religion forces).

To those who are concerned with free exercise by this country's many religions, this outcome may be quite troubling. To the extent that pluralism may be achieved in the world of judicial politics, it appropriate that different religious philosophies had their say on questions of the greatest concern to them: religious liberties.

However, in fact, we find that they have no voice, no representation at the level of the U.S. Supreme Court.

Since the myth of federal court objectivity on the basis of their lifetime appointments, has been largely discarded by those in the public law community and by legal realists, and it is widely conceded among judicial analysts that the federal courts are simply policy makers, then the question becomes: what are the appropriate policies for the federal courts to follow in these cases? It may be appropriate to offer some measure of representation to the various religious communities and groups within their areas.

To those who are more concerned with the non-establishment mandate of the First Amendment, these results may also be troubling. The objective federal bench was seemingly pulled by the various religious philosophies of its constituent judges, and thus absconded its responsibility of ensuring that a "wall of separation" exists between state and religion. Indeed, the wall is exposed as nothing but a veneer or convenient judicial metaphor which masks, as always, a highly amorphous institution with enormous power and discretion.

Chapter 12

THE U.S. SUPREME COURT IN RELIGIOUS FREEDOMS CASES 1970-1990 CHAMPION TO THE ANTI-RELIGION FORCES

ABSTRACT

This manuscript presents results from a study of two decades (1970-1990) of decision making by the U.S. Supreme Court in cases involving "religious liberties," or cases dealing with the free exercise and establishment clauses of the First Amendment to the U.S. Constitution. It test's Yarnold's (1992, 1995c) organizing framework for judicial decision making which predicts that the federal courts will be responsive to political factors in their decision making when the case involves a "major issue," (or an issue that is well-publicized and tends to divide the electorate along partisan lines); or when the case itself does not concern a major issue, but affects the interests of major organized interests in the U.S.

The results of this analysis do not nullify the main hypothesis since in cases dealing with religious liberties during the period 1970-

1990 the involvement of anti-religion groups--a political factor--was significantly related to the outcome, defined here as a "pro-religion" decision. In short, anti-religion groups were, at a statistically significant level, likely to win. Justices from the West were the only exception to the general anti-religion trend of the Court, allowing for significant pro-religion outcomes.

This project evaluates, for the period of 1970-1990, decision making by the U.S. Supreme Court in cases which concern religious liberties, protected by the First Amendment of the U.S. Constitution. Specifically, for these two decades, the analysis concentrates on cases which deal with the free exercise and establishment clauses of the First Amendment. Yarnold (1990, 1992, 1995c, N.d.a) has argued in previous research that political variables (including the partisanship of judges, the presumed desires of "judicial constituents" and the involvement of interest groups in litigation) may be significantly related to judicial decision making when the issue is a "major" issue and/or when powerful groups are interested in the outcome of the case. Since cases involving religious freedoms are major, controversial, and well-publicized cases, this analysis will serve as a good test of the organizing framework for politicized judicial decision making. Similarly, it was hypothesized that region might be significantly related to judicial outcomes when the issue considered by the courts is one with high ideological content (Yarnold 1992, 1995a, 1995c, N.d.a.). Once again, the religious freedoms cases will serve as a good test of this proposition.

In addition to examining the partisanship of judges, interest group involvement, and judicial constituents, it also divides judges into either activist judges (on the basis of their prior political and administrative positions) or non-activist and attempts to assess whether political activism is related to a more supportive posture toward religious freedom. In addition to improving the political analysis of court cases, the research includes as control variables whether the outcome in these cases is related to the judges' religious affiliations (or lack of religious faith), the ages of the judges, and their gender.

Religious Freedoms and the Federal Courts

Unlike the other "fundamental" rights contained in the First Amendment to the U.S. Constitution, including freedom of speech, press and assembly, which are arguably necessary to the functioning of a representative democracy on the basis that they serve to provide for a more enlightened and informed electorate, the free exercise and establishment clauses of the same amendment are fundamental not due to political necessity but due to historical accident: the fact that so many of the colonists had fled religious persecution in other countries. This is not meant to imply that the religious freedoms clauses of the First Amendment are secondary in any way to the others, it is instead to suggest the vital importance of religious liberty in our constitutional schema, grounded as it is in our nation's history, customs, and political culture.

Although immigrants to the United States may have often been united in their search for religious freedom, it has also been the case that religious differences in this country have led to division. Religious groups were often segregated economically, politically, socially, and even geographically (Kosmin and Lachman 1993). Underlying the debate were fundamental questions which were to guide men and women to truth, morality, justice, and knowledge of their creator. Each religious group unfortunately, tended to answer these fundamental questions with highly or slightly idiosyncratic principles. As a result, debates within the religious community were often filled with friction. To make matters worse, also entering the debate were those who insisted that they had no religious belief and did not want the state to proselytize them in any manner.

The federal courts were given the task of making order out of this disorder, through their presumably apolitical and objective interpretation of the free exercise and establishment clauses of the First Amendment. Needless to say, their interpretations of the religious freedoms clauses in specific cases has engendered even more debate, within the legal community, among legal scholars, among the press, policy makers, and the general public. Not surprisingly, there are many critics. And the criticism seems to be warranted at times, when after reviewing cases in perhaps a course on constitutional law, one finds that the rules which emanate from the federal courts in cases dealing with religious freedoms seem to change, are often unclear, conflicting, and impossible to reconcile. A frantic law student studying for a test may surmise unhappily, "perhaps there are no rules."

Although the legal community has been quite thorough in its doctrinal analysis of court cases involving religious liberties (Tribe 1988, Gey 1990, Laycock 1991, Brown 1993, Choper 1995), the same cannot be said of the public law area. To date, relatively few public law analyses of cases involving the free exercise and establishment clauses of the First Amendment have been conducted. Hence, the research is not redundant.

The research utilizes U.S. Supreme Court Cases which deal with the free exercise and establishment clauses. There are several reasons for dealing with both clauses simultaneously. The first is pragmatic: most judicial decisions which deal with religious liberties discuss both clauses. Second, from a more theoretical perspective, the free exercise and establishment clauses share a common purpose, namely protecting the liberties of religious individuals and the non-religious. Finally, it is based upon an underlying skepticism about the importance of rules, and even the existence of rules, concepts which have emerged in the public law area.

HYPOTHESES

The project draws upon Yarnold's prior work in the public law area, which has been concerned with the question of why federal court outcomes are related to political factors (including interest group involvement in litigation, the partisanship of judges, and the preferences of judicial constituencies), and to the environment, while in other types of cases political factors do not reach the level of statistical significance (Yarnold 1990a, 1990b, 1991, 1992, 1994a, 1994b, 1995a, 1995b, 1995c, N.d.a). Drawing upon this research and that of others, an organizing framework was developed (Yarnold 1992, 1995c, N.d.a) which predicts that federal courts, in spite of lifetime appointments, are likely to respond to political factors when the case in question involves a "major issue," defined as an issue that is regularly reported by the media, receives public scrutiny, and tends to conform with divisions between the Democratic and Republican parties. This, incidentally, is an adaptation of Page et. al's (1983) earlier work on congressional decision making. Hence, in Yarnold's previous research, in asylum and refugee appeals from 1980-1987 and abortion cases adjudicated during the period 1973-1990, both dealing with major issues, the outcomes were related to political factors.

In contrast, in cases dealing with international extradition, judicial outcomes were not related to the same political factors (interest group involvement, judicial constituents, and partisanship). Although these types of cases are of immense interest to certain ethnic groups in the United States, they are not well-publicized and not likely to divide the electorate along partisan lines. Hence, international extradition is not, arguably, a major issue. However, it was observed that the individuals who were subject to extradition requests were much more likely to prevail if they were linked to the IRA, while those linked to the PLO were much less likely to prevail. It was argued that the Irish lobby in the U.S. is much stronger than the Palestinian lobby. Hence, a second part of the model predicts that other cases in which judicial outcomes may be related to political factors are those which involve non-major issues, but are nevertheless of interest to major groups in the U.S.

In most of Yarnold's research, region was also included in the analysis. However, in asylum and international extradition cases, region was not significant. In contrast, in many analyses region has been found to be significantly related to judicial outcomes, for example, in environmental litigation (Wenner 1982; Wenner and Dutter 1988) and race relations cases (Richardson and Vines 1978). To reconcile these disparate findings, Yarnold (1992, 1995c) suggested that region might be most likely to be significant in cases which deal with a highly ideological issue, such as abortion. Hence, in fact, in abortion cases, region was found to be significantly related to the outcome (Yarnold 1995a, 1995b).

One of the major research objectives of this study is to test, in the context of religious liberty cases (or cases which involve the free exercise or establishment clauses), clearly cases which involve major issues, the various predictions of the organizing framework for politicized judicial decisions. Specifically, are outcomes in these cases related to "political factors" (the involvement of interest groups in litigation, judicial constituents, and the partisanship of judges)? Further, since these cases are also highly ideological, are the outcomes significantly related to region? Of course, if the predictions are unsupported by the analysis, the hope is then to fashion a new or modified one in light of the findings.

It is also anticipated that the power of the model will be enhanced by the addition of the "political activism" inquiry. In other words, it is anticipated that judges who were political activists prior to their ascent to the federal bench (they held political and/or appointive office), will decide the religious freedoms cases differently from those who were not political activists.

In addition to improving the political analysis of court cases, the research also examines other facets of the judicial environment which may also help to understand decisions in cases involving religious liberties. The dependent variable cases is whether the judicial decision is one which is pro-religion. The additional control variables which are included relate to arguably relevant factors relating to the judges including: their religious affiliations (or lack of religious belief), their ages, and their gender.

Previous Research In This Area: Findings from the District Courts and Circuit Courts of Appeals, 1970-1990

In Yarnold's review of U.S. district court outcomes in religious freedoms cases during the period 1970-1990 (Yarnold N.d.a.) it was found that four of the independent variables were related to the outcome: the gender of the judges, with male judge significantly more likely to render pro-religion decisions than female judges; the fact that the case was decided in the South or the Midwest, both regions associated with significant anti-religion outcomes; and with one political variable: the involvement of pro-religion groups in the cases. It was argued at the time that given that the courts are policy makers generally, it seemed reasonable that they acted at this level to grant some level of representation to the various pro-religion individuals and groups which appeared in these cases.

These findings were completely reversed at the level of the circuit courts of appeals. These courts, during the period 1970-1990, awarded losses to the pro-religion groups; in fact, this was the only significant variable in the analysis. Hence, the circuit courts of appeals completed reversed the policy direction of the district courts and went from broadly representative decision making which tended to be pro-religion to a policy which was elitist and anti-religion (Yarnold N.d.b.)

This analysis of the U.S. Supreme Court also attempts to discern whether the decision making is representative or elitist, whether it follows the pro-religion representative nature of the district courts, or is more likely to parallel the circuit courts of appeals as an elite, non-representative, and anti-religion policy maker.

DATA AND METHODS

Official Reporters (*U.S Reports*) were used to gather cases for this analysis. The cases included here are for two decades, from 1970-1990. The total data set is 76 U.S. Supreme Court cases decided during this period. The dependent variable in the public law analysis of court cases is: is the decision beneficial to religion (a dichotomous dependent variable)? Specifically, cases usually involve one or more religious denominations and if the decision benefits the specific denomination, then the decision is coded as "pro-religion." There is no attempt to evaluate whether the decision benefited religion in a more holistic or general sense since this would lead to great difficulty in coding the dependent variable, and lend itself to inappropriate subjective "guesses" about the extent to which religion in general is benefited by a particular judicial outcome. The more conservative approach adopted here--namely limiting the analysis to whether religious individuals and organizations who were litigants in these cases prevailed--has advantages in terms of conceptual clarity and limiting the scope of the inquiry. This conservative approach, however, also has disadvantages, since a number of cases were excluded from the analysis as they made no specific mention of a particular religious organization.

Information on interest group involvement in the cases is derived from reading the cases, which typically list the interest groups. Information on the partisan affiliations of judges, their religions (or lack of religious affiliation), their ages, and their gender is gathered from a **Judicial Staff Directory** (Brownson 1991), and from another source book, **The American Bench** (Lichterman 1978). These sources were also used to determine whether the judges are political activists, with judges gaining this designation if, in their pre-appointment activities, they held one or more elective or appointive office. Wenner's (1982; 1988) typology of region is used for coding the region variable in this analysis. The "judicial constituency" variable in these cases was measured as follows: the case was scanned to determine which religion was in issue. For example, a case involving a use of public funds for a Papal Mass was coded: Roman Catholic. Most of the cases are much more straightforward, however, involving an individual who is either filing an action or defending an action and indicates his or her religious affiliation. In other instances, as where an ordinance allows for the maintenance of a lighted cross in a public park, there is usually no specific religion involved but it will fall into the category of "general Christian." In these cases, there has been no attempt to categorize the religion. After ascertaining the religion in dispute, such as Roman Catholic, the state in which the case was adjudicated is identified. From this, the judicial constituency variable is measured as: percentage of the state population which is the religion in question. Hence if the home state of the case were Rhode Island, and the case involved Roman Catholics, a measure was made of the percentage of the population in Rhode Island in 1990 that was Catholic: 61.7% The information on the religious populations within states was derived from **Religion in Contemporary American Society**, by Kosmin and Lachman (Crown Publishers, Inc. 1993). Once again, as in the case of the dependent variable, if there is no specific mention in the case of a religious denomination, the case was excluded from the analysis.

Since the U.S. Supreme Court consists of nine justices they were each measured individually. Hence, each case was coded for all nine justices, with the individual votes of the justices. Their total votes numbered 631, but 139 of these votes had missing data, so the total data set includes 492 cases.

Since the dependent variable is dichotomous (whether the outcome is pro-religion) and there are multiple independent variables, statistical analysis involves the use of probit. Probit analysis has been employed is similar research contexts. (Segal 1984; Wenner and Dutter 1988, Yarnold 1990a, 1991a.)

The independent variables are as follows: the age of the justices at the time a decision is rendered; whether the justice is a male; whether the justice is religious; whether the justice is a political activist; whether the justice is a member of the Republican Party; are there pro-religion interest groups involved in the case; are there anti-religion interest groups in the case; what is the percentage, in 1990, of the justices state of birth, that is of the same religion that appears in the case; is the justice from the South; the Midwest; the Northeast; or the West?

Table 1

Probit Estimates for U.S. Supreme Court Cases In Religious Liberties Cases, 1970-1990

Dependent Variable: Decision Was Pro-Religion

Variable	Maximum Likelihood Error (MLE)	Standard Estimate (S.E.)	MLE/S.E.
Constant	5.97	.73	8.12
Age of Judge	- .01	.01	- 1.28
Are Judges Male?	.03	.14	.24
Are Judges Republican?	.33	.28	1.21
Are Judges Activists ?	- .12	.18	- .71
Are There Pro-	- .09	.17	- .55

Religion Groups?			
Are There Anti-Religion Groups?	- .51	.12	- 4.05*
% Judges' State Populations 1990 Same Religion As in Case	.01	.01	.95
West	.58	.32	1.82*
South	.07	.23	.30
Midwest	- .03	.18	- .17
Race (Judge White)	- .29	.34	- .89

Chi-Square = 492.7 DF = 480 P = .33
N = 285
* Significant at .05.
Note: Religion Variable (Whether judges religious) excluded since there was no variance
Note: North excluded since it was insignificant

FINDINGS

Table I shows the results of probit analysis. One deficiency with probit is that it deletes cases that have missing data, and in this analysis, missing data occurred primarily in connection with two variables: the dependent variable, namely whether the decision benefited the particular religion(s) involved in the case, and one independent variable: the religion involved in the case (for the purpose of the "judicial constituency" measure). These problems arose simply because the opinions filed by judges did not mention a religion, so they are, unavoidable. Hence, though the initial data set included 631 individual votes, 139 cases were rejected due to missing data, and 492 cases remain. There is no reason to suspect any systematic bias in the data as a result of the deletion of cases, since they were not deliberate and occurred due to chance. Hence, the remaining cases are likely representative of the total population of cases.

Only two variables are statistically significant: first, the involvement of anti-religion interest groups in the litigation, and there is an inverse relationship between pro-religion outcomes and anti-religion groups. At a statistically significant level, anti-religion groups are likely to win, in the sense that their involvement in the litigation leads to anti-religion outcomes. The only variable which tends to mitigate the general anti-religion direction of the Court was that Justices from the West were, at a level of statistical significance, likely to decide cases in a pro-religion manner.

Probit analysis generates parameter estimates through the maximum likelihood estimation (MLE) method, which assumes that the error term is normally distributed. The analysis has generated MLE estimates for each independent variable which represent the amount of change produced in the cumulative normal probability function by a one unit change in an independent variable. The MLE's divided by their standard errors approximate a normal distribution so it is possible to test whether the independent variables are significant, when controlling for other independent variables.

Hence, the MLE/SE statistic allows us to know the probability of seeing the observed results. To say that something is significant is to make the statement that, when controlling for all of the other variables, these variables still count (the significant ones). Further, it is likely that the results are not due to chance alone. An MLE/SE estimate which is significant at the .05 level means that there is only five percent or lower chance of generating these results due to chance alone.

Hence, the only victors at the level of the U.S. Supreme Court were the anti-religion groups.

One ironic note is that one of the variables, whether the justices are religious, had to dropped from the analysis since all of the justices are religious, and hence there was no variance on this variable.

DISCUSSION

The main prediction of the organizing framework for politicized judicial decision making is that in federal court cases that involve major, publicized issues, political factors will be related to the outcome. What one observes is that in cases dealing with religious liberties, the involvement of anti-religion groups in litigation—a political factor--is significantly related to the outcome in these cases. More specifically, the involvement of anti-religion groups in litigation was significantly and inversely related to a pro-religion decision by the U.S. Supreme Court in cases dealing with the free exercise and establishment clauses of the First Amendment. Hence, the most important hypothesis of the organizing framework is supported (or not rejected) in the analysis.

On a more substantive level, however, when one makes a comparison of the appeals decisions (the U.S. Supreme Court and the circuit courts of appeals) in these cases with the earlier decisions of the district courts, (Yarnold 1995c, N.d.a.), major differences emerge. And, the most important difference is that the district courts tended to give pro-religion wins to the pro-religion groups while exactly the opposite is true for the circuit courts of appeals and the U.S. Supreme Court during the two-decade period, 1970-1990. The appeals courts, at a statistically significant level, ruled against the pro-religion groups. To the extent that the district courts handed gains to the pro-religion groups which appeared before them, the circuit court of appeals reversed this policy direction, handing out losses to pro-religion groups at even higher levels than the district court granted wins. The U.S. Supreme Court granted wins only to the anti-religion groups.

Given the fact that this was the only significant variable in the circuit court of appeals cases involving religious liberties cases, to the extent that one may extrapolate some policy direction in these various courts, the district courts were favorably disposed toward pro-religion groups while the circuit courts of appeals courts overwhelmingly were opposed to the same groups. The U.S. Supreme Court went even further than the circuit courts of appeals, rewarding wins to anti-religion groups. The circuit court judges and U.S. Supreme Court justices were not closely associated with these pro-religion groups by virtue of the fact that they often came from states outside of the pro-religion groups' states of domicile.

Other differences also emerge. The circuit court of appeals courts were not linked to regional variations. District courts located in the Midwest and the South were, at a significant level, associated with anti-religion outcomes. The circuit courts of appeals were arguably not as clearly linked to their local environments as were the district courts. Neverless, regional variances do appear at the level of the U.S. Supreme Court, with Justices born in the West likely (at a statistically significant level) to enter pro-religion outcomes, however, since Justices from the West are in the minority in the Court, this factor alone did not overcome the anti-religion direction of the U.S. Supreme Court.

In the district court cases, there were also gender differences with male judges significantly more likely to enter a pro-religion decision than female judges. However, by the time we reach the level of the circuit courts of appeals, the differences are eliminated as male judges actually are more likely to enter an anti-religion decision than the female appeals judges, though this is not significant. No gender differences appear at the level of the U.S. Supreme Court.

There were two different sets of wars going on in these religious freedoms cases adjudicated by the federal district courts and circuit courts of appeals during the two decade period between 1970-1990. One war was carried on between the pro-and anti-religious groups and individuals which were involved as litigants during this period. The second type of war was between the different levels of the courts, namely district and appeals.

In terms of the war between the litigants, the federal district courts overwhelmingly favored pro-religion groups over anti-religion groups. The circuit court of appeals granted significant losses to the same pro-religion groups, and the U.S. Supreme Court went even more drastically than the appeals courts by granting wins to the anti-religion groups which appeared in these cases.

The second type of war which emerged in the religious freedoms cases adjudicated 1970-1990 was between the levels of the federal judiciary: the district courts and the appeals courts. While the district courts were characterized as populist, representative institutions, with close linkages to their regions, and with male political activist judges overwhelmingly granting victories to pro-religion groups, the circuit courts of appeals completely reversed the policy making direction of the lower federal courts. The appeals courts lost their representative nature as their links to their environments eroded and the major policy effect of the federal circuit courts of appeals was to undo the pro-religion group outcomes of the district courts. The same pro-religion groups which found victories at the level of the district court found losses at the hands of the circuit courts of appeals.

In the analysis of U.S. Supreme Court cases decided during the period 1970-1990 the same pattern applies, however, it is accentuated by the fact that the only significant winners in these cases were the anti-religion forces. Namely, the most significant variable in the Supreme Court was the anti-religious group variable, with justices granting wins to anti-religion forces, with the exception, once again of Justices born in the West.

What the U.S. Supreme Court has shown, as well as the circuit courts of appeals, is a blatant disregard for the religious freedoms of individual and pro-religion organizations. Of course, many would suggest that the anti-religion groups, such as the ACLU, simply had superior litigation resources and were more successful for this reason, however, this argument is fatuous since the pro-religion organizations, including religious denominations, have also acquired expertise in litigation.

Instead, these results are more easily understood in the broader context of politicized judicial decision-making which results from the fact that most of the Justices were political activists and obtained their promotion to the U.S. Supreme Court primarily due to their high levels of involvement in the political process. Hence, the justices assess, consciously or unconsciously, as more powerful the anti-religion lobby and so, also, the U.S. Supreme Court. Hence, the justices are skilled political survivalists, responding to the perceived power of the anti-religion groups.

So, what exactly are the implications for the pro-religion litigants who suffered repeated losses at the hands of the U.S. Supreme Court? Certainly a curtailing of their religious freedoms. So, for example the Jewish colonel in the U.S. Air Force cannot wear his yarmulke when he is in his official attire, while the Jews for Jesus organization is allowed to distribute its literature at airports. The new born/evangelicals find themselves banned in many locations from any access to the public schools, and receive little support form the U.S. Supreme Court. The Native American Indians are forever losing any right to religious practices associated with their ancestral burial grounds, as the U.S. Forest Service, with the U.S. Supreme Court's acquiescence, continue to grant developers and loggers the right to fell trees and construct roads. A Muslim prisoner is deemed to be simply without the right to weekly congregational services. State laws which prohibit mandatory work on the Sabbaths of employees are found to be unconstitutional, and conservative Christians must choose between support and their religious convictions. Of these 76 cases most (21, or 36%) involve Catholics organizations and individual litigants, most of whom lost. The Catholics cannot maintain crèches and Christmas trees in county courthouses, and repeatedly suffer financial losses as they are held by the U.S. Supreme Court not eligible for compensation for services that they have already provided to the public schools.

The victors in the U.S. Supreme Court cases were the anti-religion forces, who repeatedly won in the religious liberties cases, including, for example, the ACLU, atheist organizations, public schools and national school board organizations, various unions, Americans United for the Separation of Church and State, and NOW. Also included were public interest groups such as People for the American Way, arguing in favor of strict separation. Also involved were various business organizations who argued against any religious accommodation of their employees (such as TWA).

Chapter 13

CONCLUSION

There were two different sets of wars going on in the religious freedoms cases adjudicated by the federal district courts and appeals courts (circuit courts of appeals and U.S. Supreme Court) during the two decade period between 1970-1990. One war was carried on between the pro-and anti-religious groups and individuals which were involved as litigants during this period. The second type of war was between the different levels of the courts, namely district and appeals.

In terms of the first analysis of district court cases which dealt with either the "free exercise" or "establishment" clauses of the 1st Amendment, the federal district courts acted as a "populist" institution, with the district courts, which were staffed overwhelmingly by male, political activists, granting to local pro-religious groups favorable decisions in these cases. In short, the pro-religious groups were granted by this more "grounded" political institution decisive wins, at a statistically significant level.

Since the district court judges had most often risen through the ranks of state and local politics, indicating a high level of linkage between the district courts and their areas, it is not surprising that the district courts also rendered decisions in these cases that differed by region, at a statistically significant level. Hence, judges in the

Midwest were the most likely to render anti-religion decisions in these cases (significant), followed by the Southern judges (significant) and Northern judges (not significant). The only pro-religion outcomes were rendered by judges in the West, but this was not statistically significant.

The decisions of these district courts even had the character of the "folksy," as male judges were, at statistically significant level, more likely to render pro-religion outcomes.

In terms of the war between the litigants, the federal district courts overwhelmingly favored pro-religion groups over anti-religion groups.

The second type of war which emerged in the religious freedoms cases adjudicated 1970-1990 was between two levels of the federal judiciary: the district courts and the appeals courts (circuit courts of appeals and U.S. Supreme Court). While the district courts were characterized as populist, representative institutions, with close linkages to their regions, and with male political activist judges overwhelmingly granting victories to pro-religion groups, the appeals courts (circuit court of appeals and U.S. Supreme Court) completely reversed the policy making direction of the lower federal courts. The appeals courts lost their representative nature as their links to their environments eroded and the major policy effect of the appeals courts was to undo the pro-religion group outcomes of the district courts. The same pro-religion groups which found victories at the level of the district court found losses at the hands of the circuit courts of appeals and at the level of the U.S. Supreme Court.

The only exceptions to this general detachment of the of the appeals courts were that, at the level of the circuit courts of appeals, both Catholic and Baptist judges (note that this reverses the findings for the district courts with Baptist judges more likely to render anti-religion outcomes and only Jewish judges more inclined to take a pro-religion position in cases at a statistically significant level) were significantly more likely to decide cases in a pro-religion manner than were judges of either other denominations or no denomination. In addition, where the judges were political activists, we have also seen that they were significantly more likely to render decisions which responded to the fact that their states had a higher proportion (in terms of total population) of those of the religious denominations in these cases. Interestingly, these same patterns did not occur at the district court level; there were no significant constituency connections.

At the level of the U.S. Supreme Court, again, we find some departure from the general anti-religion stance of the appeals courts is that Justices from West were the only justices that would vote in a pro-religion manner. However, since they are so few in number, they alone are not able to counterbalance the anti-religion direction of the appeals courts (circuit courts of appeals and U.S. Supreme Court)

In contrast, at the level of the district courts, we seem a much more representative institution, there were no major differences arising between activists and non-activist district court judges in terms of their overall decisions relating to pro-religion groups, anti-religion groups, their partisanships, and the relative population of religious denominations which appeared in these cases.

The difference is again understood by viewing the district courts as the more representative institution, responding favorably to pro-religion groups and seemingly linked to their geographic regions. Since the district courts were generally representative institutions, there is no reason to expect that there would be a major difference between activist and non-activists judges in terms of their decisions in the religious freedoms cases.

The non-representative character of the appeals courts was mitigated , at the level of the federal circuit courts of appeals by the fact that Catholic and Baptist judges tended to render pro-religion decisions and by the fact that political activists responded significantly to their judicial constituencies; in other words, their decisions in these cases were positively linked to the religions which appeared in the religious freedoms cases, with activist appeals judges rendering a pro-religion decision when the religions which appeared in these cases were significant forces in the judges' states due to the fact that they constituted a relatively large proportion of the total populations of the states.

More precisely, the only representative inclinations of the federal circuit courts of appeals were exhibited by Catholic and Baptist judges (who rendered pro-religion decisions) and by political activists among the appeals courts, who responded to a significant judicial constituency in the cases, namely, the more important religious denominations which appeared in the religious freedoms cases in the sense that they were a significant players in the judges' states in terms of their population relative to the total population of the states.

At the level of the U.S. Supreme Court, the only pro-religion representation was offered by Western judges, who were a minority and weak voice.

Yet, the main observation still holds: that the district court judges in the religious freedoms cases were the more representative players, responding to their regions, granting to pro-religion groups significant victories, and even responding to gender, with male judges more inclined to grant pro-religion decisions than female judges.

Of course, it is almost unnecessary at this point to make an observation which seems to be almost a truism, namely, that the divergent outcomes in district and appeals courts cases, their differing policy directions, and even the extent to which they play a "representative" role, demonstrate once again even more forcefully that the federal courts, are simply another political, policy making institution.

THEORETICAL QUESTIONS

As stated in the "Introduction," the project draws upon Yarnold's prior work in the public law area, which has been concerned with the question of why federal court outcomes are related to political factors (including interest group involvement in litigation, the partisanship of judges, and the preferences of judicial constituencies), and to the environment, while in other types of cases political factors do not reach the level of statistical significance (Yarnold 1990a, 1990b, 1991, 1992, 1994a, 1994b 1995, N.d.). Drawing upon Yarnold's research and that of others, a general theory of public law was developed (Yarnold 1992, 1995) which predicts that federal courts, in spite of lifetime appointments, are likely to respond to political factors when the case in question involves a major issue that is well-publicized and tends to divide the electorate along partisan lines. This, incidentally, is an adaptation of Page et. al's (1983) earlier work on congressional decision making. Hence, in Yarnold's previous research, asylum and refugee appeals from 1980-1987 and abortion cases adjudicated during the period 1973-1990, both dealing with major issues, the outcomes were related to political factors.

In contrast, in cases dealing with international extradition, judicial outcomes were not related to the same political factors (interest group involvement, judicial constituents, and partisanship). Although these types of cases are of immense interest to certain ethnic groups in the United States, they are not well-publicized and not likely to divide the electorate along partisan lines. Hence, international extradition is not, arguably, a major issue. However, it was observed that the individuals who were subject to extradition requests were much more likely to prevail if they were linked to the IRA, while those linked to the PLO were much less likely to prevail. It was argued that the Irish lobby in the U.S. is much stronger than the Palestinian lobby. Hence, a second part of the model predicts that other cases in which judicial outcomes may be related to political factors are those which involve non-major issues, but are nevertheless of interest to major groups in the U.S.

In most of the Yarnold's research, region was also included in the analysis. However, in asylum and international extradition cases, region was not significant. In contrast, in many analyses region has been found to be significantly related to judicial outcomes, for example, in environmental litigation (Wenner 1982; Wenner and Dutter 1988) and race relations cases (Richardson and Vines 1978). To reconcile these disparate findings, Yarnold (1995) suggested that region might be most likely to be significant in cases which deal with a highly ideological issue, such as abortion. Hence, in fact, in abortion cases, region was found to be significantly related to the outcome (Yarnold 1995).

One of the major research objectives of this study is to test, in the context of religious liberty cases (or cases which involve the free exercise or establishment clauses), clearly cases which involve major issues, the various predictions of the general theory of public law.

Specifically, are outcomes in these cases related to "political factors" (the involvement of interest groups in litigation, judicial constituents, and the partisanship of judges)? Further, since these cases are also highly ideological, are the outcomes significantly related to region? Of course, if the model is unsupported by the analysis, the hope is then to fashion a new or modified one in light of the new findings.

It is also anticipated that the power of the model will be enhanced by the addition of the "political activism" inquiry. In other words, it is anticipated that judges which were political activists prior to their ascent to the federal bench (they held political and/or appointive office), will decide the religious freedoms cases differently from those who were not political activists, although there is no specific prediction at this point about the direction of the relationship (that is, whether they will be more of less sympathetic to "religion" than their non-activist counterparts).

In an effort to further understand politically activist judges, the analysis will also evaluate whether the activists are more likely than the non-activists to render decisions which favor interest groups, are responsive to judicial constituents, and are highly partisan.

In addition to improving the political analysis of court cases, the research will also examine other facets of the judicial environment which may also help to understand decisions in cases involving religious liberties. The dependent variable in all cases is whether the judicial decision is one which is pro-religion. The additional factors which will be included relate to arguably relevant factors relating to the judges including: their religious affiliations (or lack of religious belief), their ages, and their gender.

THEORETICAL CONTRIBUTIONS: THE FINAL TESTS

In Chapter 4, in the analysis of district court cases, we find that the main prediction of the organizing framework or "general theory of public law" for politicized judicial decision making is that in federal court cases that involve major, publicized issues, political factors will be related to the outcome. What one observes is that in cases dealing with religious liberties, the involvement of pro-religion groups in litigation--a political factor--is significantly related to the outcome in these cases. More specifically, the involvement of pro-religion groups in litigation was significantly related to a pro-religion decision by the federal district courts in cases dealing with the free exercise and establishment clauses of the First Amendment. Hence, the most important hypothesis of the organizing framework is supported (or not rejected) in the analysis.

The political activism, measure, however, does not add to our understanding of the political dynamics of the federal judiciary. Federal district judges who were classified as political activists due to the fact that they held one or more elective and/or appointive office prior to their ascension to the federal bench were slightly more likely to render a pro-religion decision, but this variable is not significant.

Two of the regional variables were significantly related to the outcomes in the district court cases. Courts in the West were the only courts which tended to have pro-religion outcomes, but this was not significant. All other regions recorded anti-religion outcomes, including the Northeast (not significant), the South (significant), and the Midwest (significant).

Also interesting is the fact that male district judges were significantly more likely to render a pro-religion decision than female judges. Hence, an apparent gender difference arises in these cases. Further research is called for to evaluate why this gender difference might arise. One possibility is that most of the female judges tend to be relatively new additions to the federal bench. Perhaps they are just beginning their acculturation or assimilation into the lower federal bench and once this process is complete, they will resemble more in their decision making their male counterparts on the bench.

With regard to the outcomes of the appeals courts in religious freedoms cases, the main prediction of the "organizing framework" or "general theory" for politicized judicial decision making is that in federal court cases that involve major, publicized issues, political factors will be related to the outcome. What one observes is that in appeals cases dealing with religious liberties, the involvement of pro-religion groups in litigation--a political factor--is significantly related to the outcome in these cases. More specifically, the involvement of pro-religion groups in litigation was significantly and inversely related to a pro-religion decision by the federal circuit courts of appeals in cases dealing with the free exercise and establishment clauses of the First Amendment. Hence, the most important hypothesis of the organizing framework is supported (or not rejected) in the analysis. At the level of the Supreme Court, this finding is duplicated, as the U.S. Supreme Court grants wins to the anti-religion forces.

On a more substantive level, however, when one makes a comparison of the appeals decisions in these cases with the earlier decisions of the district courts, (Yarnold 1995c, N.d.), major differences emerge. And, the most important difference is that the district courts tended to give pro-religion wins to the pro-religion groups while exactly the opposite is true for the appeals (both circuit courts of appeals and U.S. Supreme Court) during the two-decade period, 1970-1990. The appeals courts, at a statistically significant level, ruled against the pro-religion groups, or in favor of anti-religion groups. To the extent that the district courts handed gains to the pro-religion groups which appeared before them, the appeals courts reversed this policy direction, handing out losses to pro-religion groups at even higher levels than the district court granted wins.

Given the fact that this was the only significant variable in the appeals cases involving religious liberties cases, to the extent that one may extrapolate some policy direction in these various courts, the district courts were favorably disposed toward pro-religion groups while the appeals courts overwhelmingly were opposed to the same groups. The appeals judges were not closely associated with these pro-religion groups by virtue of the fact that they often came from states outside of the pro-religion groups' states of domicile.

Other differences also emerge. The appeals courts were not linked to regional variations. Judges in the North, South, and West tended to rule in a pro-religion way, while courts in the Midwest tended to rule in an anti-religion manner, but none of these are significant. District courts located in the Midwest and the South were, at a significant level, associated with anti-religion outcomes. The circuit courts of appeals were arguably not as clearly linked to their local environments as were the district courts.

The only exception to the lack of links between region and decisions of the appeals courts is that Supreme Court justices from the West tended to grant wins to pro-religion litigants.

In the district court cases, there were also gender differences with male judges significantly more likely to enter a pro-religion decision than female judges. However, by the time we reach the level of the appeals level, gender differences are eliminated.

Another interesting finding was in the analysis of appeals court judges, where it was found that activist judges did decide cases in a manner distinct from non-activist judges, and that, specifically, of the possible variables, activist judges responded differentially on the judicial constituency variable, namely the extent to which local religious groups appearing in appeals court cases are well-represented in terms of overall state population. Hence, the political activism measure did make an important contribution to our understanding of politicized judicial decision making. This difference did not emerge at the level of the Supreme Court.

REFERENCES

Atiyah, P.S. and Robert S. Summers 1987. *Form and Substance in Anglo-American Law*. New York: Oxford University Press.

Austin, T.L. 1980. "The Influence of Legal and Extra-Legal Factors on Sentencing Dispositions in Rural, Semi-Rural and Urban Counties." Ann Arbor, Michigan: University Microfilms International.

Baum, Lawrence 1989. *The Supreme Court*. Washington, D.C.: Congressional Quarterly, Inc.

Beiser, Edward N. "The Rhode Island Supreme Court: A Well-Integrated Political System." In *American Court Systems*, eds. S. Goldman and A. Sarat, pp. 470-79. San Francisco: W.H. Freeman and Company.

Blank, Robert H. 1984. "Judicial Decision Making and Biological Fact: Roe v. Wade and the Unresolved Question of Fetal Viability." *Western Political Quarterly* 37: 584-602.

Bolce, Louis 1988. "Abortion and Presidential Elections: The Impact of Public Perceptions of Party and Candidate Positions." *Presidential Studies Quarterly* 18: 815-29.

Brown, Rebecca L. 1993. "Tradition and Insight." *Yale Law Journal* 103: 177.

Brownson, Ann L. 1991. *1991 Judicial Staff Directory*. Mount Vernon, Virginia: Staff Directories, Ltd.

Caldeira, Gregory A. 1981. "Judicial Incentives." In *Courts, Law, and Judicial Processes*, ed. S.S. Ulmer, pp. 143-49. New York: Free Press.

____________________, 1987. "Public Opinion and the U.S. Supreme Court: FDR's Court-Packing Plan." *American Political Science Review* 81: 1139-54.

Caldeira, Gregory A. and James L. Gibson 1992. "The Etiology of Public Support for the Supreme Court." *American Journal of Political Science* 36: 635-664.

Carp, R. and C. Rowland. 1983. *Policy Making And Politics In The Federal District Courts*. Knoxville: University of Tennessee Press.

Casper, Jonathan D. 1981. The Public Defender: Man in the Middle." In *Courts, Law, And Judicial Processes*, ed. S.S. Ulmer, pp. 87-94. New York: Free Press.

Choper, Jesse H. 1995. *Securing Religious Liberty*. Chicago: University of Chicago Press.

Cook, Beverly B. 1977. "Public Opinion and Federal Judicial Policy." *Journal Of Political Science* 2: 567-600.

Cook, Beverly B. 1981. "Sentencing Behavior of Federal Judges--Draft Cases--1972." In S. Ulmer, ed., *Courts, Law, And Judicial Processes*, pp. 462-469. New York: Free Press.

Cummings, Milton C., Jr. and David Wise 1985. *Democracy Under Pressure*. San Diego: Harcourt, Brace, Javonovich.

Danelski, David J. 1978. "The Influence of the Chief Justice in the Decisional Process of the Supreme Court." In *American Court Systems*, eds. S. Goldman and A. Sarat, pp. 506-19. San Francisco: W.H. Freeman and Company.

Danelski, David J. 1981. "Values as Variables in Judicial Decision Making." In *Courts, Law, And Judicial Processes*, ed. S.S. Ulmer, pp. 397-402. New York: Free Press.

De Turo, Doreen and Nancy Barnes 1985. Editors, *The American Bench: Judges of the Nation*. Sacramento: Reginald Bishop Forster & Associates, Inc.

Dolbeare, Kenneth M. 1978. "The Federal District Courts and Urban Public Policy." In *American Court Systems*, eds. S. Goldman and A. Sarat, pp. 535-545. San Francisco: W. H. Freeman and Company.

Elazar, D. 1972. *American Federalism: A View From The States*. New York: Thomas Y. Crowell Company.

Epstein, Lee 1985. *Conservatives In Court*. Knoxville: University of Tennessee Press.

Epstein, Lee and C.K. Rowland 1991. "Debunking the Myth of Interest Group Invincibility in the Courts, American Political Science Review, 85: 205-217.

Epstein, Lee, Thomas G. Walker, and Dixon, William J. 1989. "The Supreme Court and Criminal Justice Disputes: A Neo-Institutional Perspective." *American Journal of Political Science* 33: 825-41.

Feldman, Stanley 1988. "Structure and Consistency in Public Opinion: the Role of Core Beliefs and Values." *American Journal of Political Science* 32: 416-440.

Frank, Jerome 1949. *Courts on Trial: Myth and Reality in American Justice*. Princeton:, New Jersey: Princeton University Press.

Frank, Jerome 1963. *Law and the Modern Mind*. Anchor Books.

Frank, Jerome 1978. "Facts are Guesses." In *American Court Systems*, eds. S. Goldman and A. Sarat, pp. 310-316. San Francisco: W.H. Freeman and Company.

Franklin, Charles H. and Liane C. Kosaki 1989. "Republican Schoolmaster: The U.S. Supreme Court, Public Opinion, And Abortion." *American Political Science Review* 83: 751-71.

Galanter, M. 1974. "Why the 'Haves' Come Out Ahead: Speculation on the Limits of Social Change." *Law And Society Review* 9: 85-160.

Galanter, M. 1978. "Who Wins?" In *American Court Systems*, eds. S. Goldman and A Sarat. San Francisco: W.H. Freeman and Company.

Gey, Steven G. 1990. "Why Is Religion Special? Reconsidering the Accommodation of Religion under the Religion Clauses of the First Amendment." *University of Pittsburgh Law Review* 52: 75.

Gibson, James L. 1977. "Discriminant Functions, Role Orientations and Judicial Behavior: Theoretical and Methodological Linkages." *Journal Of Politics* 37: 917-36.

Giles, M.W. and Walker, T.G. 1978. "Judicial Policy-Making and Southern School Segregation." In *American Court Systems*, eds. S. Goldman and A. Sarat, pp. 386-95. San Francisco: W. H. Freeman and Company.

Glick, H.R. 1983. *Courts, Politics And Justice*. New York: McGraw-Hill, Inc.

Goldman, Sheldon 1975. "Voting Behavior on the U.S. Court of Appeals." *American Political Science Review* 69: 491-506.

Goldman, Sheldon 1978. "Voting Behavior on the United State Courts of Appeals Revisited." In *American Court Systems*, eds. S. Goldman and A. Sarat, pp. 396-411. San Francisco: W.H. Freeman and Company.

Gryski, Gerald S., Eleanor C. Main and William J. Dixon 1986. "Models of State Court High Decision Making in Sex Discrimination Cases." *Journal Of Politics* 48: 143-55.

Haire, Susan and Donald R. Songer 1990. "A Multivariate Model of Voting on the United States Courts of Appeals." Prepared for delivery at the 1990 Annual Meeting of the Midwest Political Science Association, the Palmer House Hotel, Chicago, Illinois, April 7, 1990.

Hall, Jeffrey A. 1987. "A Recommended Approach to Bail in International Extradition Cases." *Michigan Law Review* 86: 599.

Hart, H.A.L. 1961. *The Concept of Law*. London: Oxford University Press.

Helton, A.C. 1984. "Political Asylum Under the 1980 Refugee Act: An Unfulfilled Promise." *University Of Michigan Law Reference* 17: 243-264.

Helton, A.C. 1985. "The Proper Role of Discretion in Political Asylum Determinations." *San Diego Law Review* 22: 999-1020.

Hofferbert, Richard I. 1974. *The Study Of Public Policy*. New York: Bobbs-Merrill Company, Inc.

Howard, J. Woodward, Jr. 1978. "Role Perceptions and Behavior in Three U.S. Courts of Appeals." In *American Court Systems*, eds. S. Goldman and A. Sarat, pp. 480-89. San Francisco: W.H. Freeman and Company.

Jacob, Herbert 1981. "Attorneys for the Public." In *Courts, Law, and Judicial Processes*, ed. S.S. Ulmer, pp. 82-87. New York: Free Press.

Kairys, David 1990. *The Politics of Law: A Progressive Critique*. Editor, revised second edition. New York: Pantheon Books.

Kelman, Mark 1987. *A Guide To Critical Legal Studies*. Cambridge: Harvard University Press.

Kemp, Kathleen A., Robert A. Carp, and David W. Brady 1978. "The Supreme Court and Social Change: The Case of Abortion." *Western Political Quarterly* 31: 19-31.

Kennedy, Duncan and Karl E. Klare 1984. "A Bibliography of Critical Legal Studies." *Yale Law Journal* 94: 461-463.

Kennedy, Duncan 1986. "Freedom and Constraint in Adjudication: A Critical Phenomenology." *Journal of Legal Education* 36: 518-562.

Kosmin, Barry A. and Seymour P. Lachman, editors, 1993. *One Nation Under God: Religion in Contemporary American Society.* New York: Crown Trade Paperbacks.

Kritzer, H. 1978. "Political Correlates of the Behavior of Federal District Judges." *Journal Of Politics* 40: 25-57.

Laycock, Douglas 1991. "'Noncoercive' Support for Religion: Another False Claim About the Establishment Clause." *Val. Law Review* 26: 37.

Levin, Martin A. 1978. "Urban Politics and Judicial Behavior". In *American Court Systems*. eds. S. Goldman and A. Sarat, pp. 338-347. San Francisco: W.H. Freeman and Company.

Lichterman, Nancy 1978. Editor, *The American Bench: Judges of the Nation*. Minnesota: Reginald Bishop Forster & Associates, Inc.

LLewellyn, Karl 1930. *Cases and Materials on Sales.* Chicago: Callaghan & Company.

Llewellyn, Karl 1931. "Some Realism about Realism." *Harvard Law Review* 44: 1222, 1237.

Marshall. Thomas R. 1989. *Public Opinion and the Supreme Court.* Boston: Unwin Hyman, Inc.

Miller, W. and D. Stokes 1963. "Constituency Influence in Congress." *American Journal Of Political Science* 57: 45-56, 1963.

Murphy, Cornelius, F., Jr. 1978. *Modern Legal Philosophy.* Pitssburgh: Duquesne University Press.

Murphy, Walter F. 1981. "Courts as Small Groups." In *Courts, Law, And Judicial Processes*, ed. S.S. Ulmer, pp. 363-67. New York: Free Press.

Myers, M. 1987. ""Economic Inequality and Discrimination in Sentencing." *Social Forces*: 65(3): 746-766.

Myers, M. 1988. "Social Background and the Sentencing Behavior of Judges." *Criminology* 26(4): 649-73.

Nagel, I. and J. Hagan 1983. "Gender and Crime: Offense Patterns and Criminal Court Sanctions." *Crime And Justice: Annual Review Of Research* 4: 91-144.

Nagel, Stuart S. 1961. "Political Party Affiliation and Judges' Decisions." *American Political Science Review* 55: 843-850.

O'Connor, K. 1980. *Women's Organizations Use Of The Courts*. Lexington: Lexington Books.

Page, B.I., Shapiro, R.Y., Gronke, P.W. and R.M. Rosenberg. 1984. "Constituency, Party, and Representation in Congress." *Public Opinion Quarterly* 48: 741-756.

Pritchett, C. Herman. 1978. "Voting Behavior on the United States Supreme Court." In *American Court Systems*, eds. S. Goldman and A. Sarat. pp. 424-431. San Francisco: W.H. Freeman and Company.

Richardson, R.J. and K.N. Vines. 1978. "Judicial Constituencies: The Politics of Structure." In *American Court Systems*, eds. S. Goldman and A. Sarat, pp. 348-353. San Francisco: W.H. Freeman and Company.

Saltman, Michael 1991. *The Demise of the 'Reasonable Man.'* New Brunswick: Transaction Publishers.

Schattshneider, E.E. 1960. *The Semisovereign People*. New York: Holt, Reinhart and Winston.

Schubert, G. 1965. *The Judicial Mind*. Evanston: Northwestern University Press.

Segal, J. 1984. "Predicting Supreme Court Cases Probabilistically: The Search and Seizure Cases 1962-1981." *American Political Science Review* 78: 891-900.

Segal, Jeffrey A. 1985. "Measuring Change on the Supreme Court: Examining Alternative Models." *American Journal Of Political Science* 29: 461-79.

Segal, Jeffrey A. and Albert D. Cover 1989. "Ideological Values and the Votes of U.S Supreme Court Justices." *American Political Science Review* 83: 557-563.

Segal, J.A., Cameron, C.M., and Cover, A.D., 1992. "A Spatial Model of Roll Call Voting: Senators, Constituents, Presidents, and Interest Groups in Supreme Court Confirmations." *American Journal of Political Science* 36: 96-121.

Shapiro, Martin, 1993. "Public Law and Judicial Politics." In *Political Science: The State of the Discipline II*, editor, Ada W. Finifter, pages 365-381. Washington, D.C.: the American Political Science Association.

Sheehan, R.S., W. Mishler, And D.S. Songer 1992. "Ideology, Status, and the Differential Success of Direct Parties Before the Supreme Court." *American Political Science Review* 86: 464-71.

Songer, Donald R. and Sue Davis 1990. "The Impact of Party and Region on Voting Decisions in the U.S Courts of Appeals, 1955-86." *Western Political Quarterly* 43: 317-44.

Songer, Donald R. and Susan Haire 1992. "Integrating Alternative Approaches to the Study of Judicial Voting: Obscenity Cases in the U.S. Courts of Appeals." *American Journal of Political Science* 36: 963-82.

Songer, Donald R. and Reginald S. Sheehan 1992. "Who Wins on Appeal? Upperdogs and Underdogs in the United States Courts of Appeals." *American Journal of Political Science* 36: 235-58.

Spaeth, Harold J. 1981. "The Attitudes and Values of Supreme Court Justices." In *Courts, Law, And Judicial Processes*, ed. S.S. Ulmer, pp. 387-397. New York: Free Press.

Spencer, C.C. 1978. "Sexual Assault: The Second Victimization." In *Women, The Courts, And Equality*, eds. L. Crites and W. Hepperle. Beverly Hills: Sage Publications.

Spohn, C., Gruhl, J. and Susan Welch 1981-1982. "The Effects of Race on Sentencing: A Re-Examination of an Unsettled Question." *Law And Society Review* 16(1): 71-88.

Sprague, J.D. 1968. *Voting Patterns Of The U.S. Supreme Court*. New York: Bobbs-Merrill Co.

Stokes, D. 1963. "Spatial Models of Party Competition" *American Political Science Review* 57: 368-377.

Tanenhaus, J. 1961. "Supreme Court Attitudes Toward Federal Administrative Agencies 1947-1956--An Application of Social Science Methods to the Study of Judicial Process." *Vanderbilt Law Review* 14: 482-501.

Tanenhaus, J., Schick, M., Muraskin, M., and D. Rosen 1981. "The Supreme Court's Certiorari Jurisdiction: Cue Theory." In *Courts, Law, And Judicial Processes*, ed. S. Ulmer, pp. 273-283. New York: Free Press.

Tate, C. Neal 1981. "Personal Attribute Models of the Voting Behavior of United States Supreme Court Justices: Liberalism in Civil Liberties and Economic Decisions, 1946-1978." *American Political Science Review* 75: 355-67.

C. Neal Tate and Roger Handberg 1991. "Time Binding and Theory Building in Personal Attribute Models of Supreme Court Voting Behavior, 1916-88." *American Journal of Political Science* 35: 460-80.

Tribe, Laurence H. 1988. *American Constitutional Law*. (2nd Edition)

Tushnet, Mark 1986. "Critical Legal Studies: An Introduction to its Origins and Underpinnings." *Journal of Legal Education* 36: 505-517.

Ulmer, S. Sidney 1981. *Courts, Law, and Judicial Processes*. New York: Free Press.

Ungs, T.D. and L.R. Bass 1972. "Judicial Role Perceptions: A Q-Technique Study of Ohio Judges." *Law And Society Review* 6: 343-366.

Unnever, J. and L. Hembroff 1988. "The Prediction of Racial/Ethnic Sentencing Disparities: An Expectation States Approach." *Journal Of Research In Crime And Delinquency* 25: 53-82.

Vines, Kenneth N. 1963. "The Role of Circuit Courts of Appeal in the Federal Judicial Process: a Case Study." *Midwest Journal Of Political Science* 7: 305-319.

Vines, Kenneth N. 1978. "Federal District Judges and Race Relations Cases in the South." in *American Court Systems*, eds. S. Goldman and A. Sarat, pp. 376-385. San Francisco: W.H. Freeman and Company.

Vose, C. 1959. *Caucasians Only*. Berkeley: Knopf.

Wall, D. 1985. "Michigan Supreme Court and Court of Appeals Election." Paper presented at Midwest Political Science Association.

Wenner, Lettie M. 1982. *The Environmental Decade In Court*. Bloomington: Indiana University Press.

Wenner, Lettie and Lee Dutter 1988. "Contextual Influences on Court Outcomes." *Western Political Quarterly* 41: 115-134.

Yarnold, Barbara M. 1988. "United States Refugee and Asylum Policy: Factors that Impact Legislative, Administrative and Judicial Decisions." Ph.D. diss. University of Illinois at Chicago.

Yarnold, Barbara M. 1990a. "Federal Court Outcomes In Asylum-Related Appeals 1980-1987: A Highly 'Politicized' Process." *Policy Sciences*. 23 (4) (November 1990): 291-306.

Yarnold, Barbara M. 1990b. *Refugees Without Refuge: Formation And Failed Implementation Of U.S. Political Asylum Policy In The 1980s*. Lanham, Maryland: University Press of America.

Yarnold, Barbara M. 1990c. "The Refugee Act of 1980 and the De-Politicization of Refugee/Asylum Admissions: An Example of Failed Policy Implementation." *American Politics Quarterly* 18(4) (October 1990): 527-36.

Yarnold, Barbara M. 1991a. *International Fugitives: A New Role For The International Court Of Justice*. New York, New York: Praeger Publishers, Inc. (an imprint of Greenwood Publishing Group).

Yarnold, Barbara M. 1995c. "A General Theory of Public Law." *Legal Studies Forum*, 19: 317-340.

Yarnold, Barbara M. 1995-1996. Ethnic Politics in U.S. Courts: U.S. District Court Outcomes in International Extradition Cases 1932-1990. 5: In Depth: 23-52.

Yarnold, Barbara M. N.d. "Factors Related to Outcomes In Religious Freedoms Cases, Federal District Courts: 1970-1990." *Justice System Journal*, forthcoming.

INDEX

R

U